THE CAMBRIDGE MISCELLANY

XIV

SHAKESPEARE

T0352049

SHAKESPEARE

BY

GEORGE SAINTSBURY

WITH

AN APPRECIATION

BY

HELEN WADDELL

CAMBRIDGE

AT THE UNIVERSITY PRESS

1934

CAMBRIDGE UNIVERSITY PRESS
Cambridge, New York, Melbourne, Madrid, Cape Town,
Singapore, São Paulo, Delhi, Tokyo, Mexico City

Cambridge University Press
The Edinburgh Building, Cambridge CB2 8RU, UK

Published in the United States of America by
Cambridge University Press, New York

www.cambridge.org
Information on this title: www.cambridge.org/9781107624290

First published 1934
First paperback edition 2011

A catalogue record for this publication is available from the British Library

ISBN 978-1-107-62429-0 Paperback

PUBLISHER'S NOTE

This book contains the two chapters on Shakespeare contributed by the late George Saintsbury to the fifth volume of the *Cambridge History of English Literature*. A few footnotes have been added.

GEORGE SAINTSBURY

GEORGE SAINTSBURY was born on 23 October, 1845, at Southampton: he died at Bath on 28 January, 1933, and was brought for burial to the place of his birth. He had lived within twelve years of a century: like Dryden and like Dr Johnson, the builder-oak of the criticism of his time. As insular in one sense as the Venerable Bede (for though a great walker he was no traveller), he had like him the *potestas orbis terrarum*, at any rate of the lands the Romans knew. And like him too, 'in every generation he speaks familiarly'. There is no fashion so dead as that of the day before yesterday, and the yesterday between 1914 and 1918 was a gap that few men of seventy could bridge. But something in his integrity, the magnanimity and ripeness and obstinacy of his mind, his quick ironic concern for the new world about him, his awareness—in the phrase which he used to illumine the darkness of Swift— of 'the accepted hells beneath', his faith in a *civitas Dei* that honourable men might still inherit: these made his name a stronghold, an assurance that some things could not be shaken. 'That choleric and heavenly temper of thine', wrote Peter of Celle to John of Salisbury, 'is gayest in thine afflictions, puts forth leaves in the frost': and those who saw him in the Augustan twilight of the house of his last inhabiting, a solitary indomitable figure with straggling grey hair and black skull-cap, gaunt as Merlin and islanded in a fast-encroaching sea of books, came out from him with some understanding of Boethius' definition of eternity—'whatsoever comprehendeth and possesseth the whole fulness of life here and now, to which naught of the future is lacking, and from which naught of the past hath flowed away'. The miseries of old age and the slow

7

oncoming of death had no dominion over that free spirit.

It was his habit to commend Gibbon as one who could regard his subject from a vantage-ground of twenty centuries: but for himself, the centuries were not so much a vantage-ground, as a continuation of his own experience. He read, in Milton's phrase, 'as if alive in every age'. Whether the book before him is Petronius Arbiter's *Satyricon* or Norman Douglas's *South Wind*, he speaks of it as its contemporary. It might seem impossible that a man of his extreme idiosyncrasy and vigorous prejudice should have been the most catholic critic of his time, most profoundly the 'Understander' whom Ben Jonson in preface after preface invoked in vain. Yet this High Churchman and High Tory refused to join the chorus of censure on the 'scrannel pipes' outburst in *Lycidas*: 'the supremacy of expression and phrase and verse remains—the discord and declension, even to those who find them such, are in the sentiment only'. The 'fits and squalls of moral darkness' in Hazlitt never overshadowed for him 'the abiding intellectual light', though it is plain that he becomes embarrassed by 'a kind of shabbiness' in Hazlitt's handling of his affairs: and he was the first to rehabilitate Leigh Hunt, in spite of all those shifts and meannesses against which, as a *Times* reviewer once put it, 'the King of critics might have roared a noble indignation'. 'The man could write': the neck-verse saved many a hanging. If it did not wholly save Sterne, it was because he offended in the one particular that turned Saintsbury's ink to vitriol. Not frank indecency: he could dismiss that in his beloved Rabelais as 'a time-deodorised dunghill by the roadside, not beautiful, but negligible'. But the snigger he could not away with: and if Sterne is damned, it is because a 'perfect literary artist' has crystallised the snigger in English prose.

8

He had indeed to defend himself more than once for his catholicity,

> Je voudrais boire tout le vin
> Et baiser tout le monde.

For the critic's baptism, he wrote, *manet oceanus*: and the Unpardonable Sin to him was 'enquiring of a work of art whether it has done, not what the artist meant it, but what the critic wanted it, to do....The religion of literature is a sort of Pantheism: you never know when the presence of the Divine *may* show itself, though you must know where it has shown. And you must never forbid it to show itself, anyhow or anywhere'. Like his favourite Longinus, his final test was the literal *transport*, the taking of a man out of himself: and it might be with the resistless sweep of

> All night the dreadless Angel, unpursu'd,

or the jogging homeward trot to

> The table-flap, the mutton-bone, and Mary.

In either instance, the man has done what he set out to do. 'Wordsworth can...write the most detestable doggerel and platitude. But when anyone who knows what poetry is reads—

> Our noisy years seem moments in the being
> Of the eternal silence,

he sees that, quite independently of the meaning...there is one note added to the articulate music of the world.... He leaves Wordsworth, he goes straight into the middle of the eighteenth century, and he sees Thomson with his hands in his dressing-gown pockets biting at the peaches, and hears him between the mouthfuls murmuring—

> So when the shepherd of the Hebrid Isles
> Placed far amid the melancholy main,

and there is another note, as different as possible in kind

and yet alike, struck for ever.... In this matter, as in all matters that are worth handling at all, we come of course *ad mysterium*. Why certain combinations of letters, sounds, cadences, should almost without the aid of meaning... produce this effect of poetry on men, no man can say. But they do.'

Saintsbury, said his critics, 'writ no language'. It was one of the many contradictions in him—contradictions that made his very existence extremely delightful to his friends—that he whose main preoccupation was form in verse or prose, and whose first essay, *Baudelaire*, preached his lifelong and unpopular doctrine of style before subject, should himself write like the scour of a river in spate, allusion tumbling on allusion, parenthesis rammed within parenthesis, reckless to reject the straws and faggots that his headlong thought swept up on its course. But this very unselfconsciousness, this possession of the man by the subject, had its rewards. The range of his style is enormous. There was an adroit and mischievous gravity, of which these chapters on Shakespeare are sufficient evidence: 'The uncertainty of the poet's birthday is one of the best known things about him'.... 'But the nature of commentators abhors a vacuum.' There was an extraordinary balance and epigraphic quality, seen at its height in the preface to his *Specimens of English Prose Style*, on the writers of the early eighteenth century: 'They were unrivalled in vigour, not easily to be beaten in sober grace, abundantly capable of wit, but as a rule they lacked magnificence.... Addison's renowned homilies on death and tombs and a future life have rather an unrivalled decency... than solemnity in the higher sense of the term'. Here, his style has itself this unrivalled decency: but on poetry, it can at times reach to magnificence. On Dryden: 'the inimitable ring which distinguishes his verse from all others—the ring as of a great bronze coin thrown down on marble'. On Shakespeare's Sonnets, after a characteristically contemptuous handling of the theories, biographical and other, which account for them: 'All these theories and others are possible: none is proved: and for the literary purpose, none is really important. What is important is that Shakespeare has here caught up the sum of love and uttered it as no poet has before or since, and that in so doing he carried poetry— that is to say, the passionate expression in verse of the sensual and intellectual facts of life—to a pitch which it had never previously reached in English, and which it has never outstepped since. The coast line of humanity must be wholly altered, the sea must change its nature, the moon must draw it in different ways, before that tide-mark is passed'. His own tide-mark is reached in his criticism of Donne: 'But it is not here [in satire] that we find the true Donne: it was not this province of the universal monarchy of wit that he ruled with the most unshackled sway. The provinces that he did so rule were quite other: strange frontier regions, uttermost isles where sensuality, philosophy, and devotion meet...'. 'Behind every image, every ostensible thought of his, there are vistas and backgrounds of other thoughts dimly vanishing, with glimmers in them here and there into the depths of the final enigmas of life and soul. Passion and meditation, the two avenues into this region of doubt and dread, are tried by Donne in the two sections respectively, and of each he has the key. Nor, as he walks in them with eager or solemn tread, are light and music wanting, the light the most unearthly that ever played about a poet's head, the music not the least heavenly that he ever caught and transmitted to his readers.'

For Saintsbury, there was no poet, and hardly any

writer, like Donne. And the spiritual and sensual kinship between these two men, the poet and his first discoverer, had its counterpart in the circumstances of their lives. Both were of a high pride and in their youth of towering ambition, and both were checked and frustrated of what they had judged to be their vocation, courtly diplomacy for one, 'Academe' at Oxford for the other. Both were denied security and reputation through the best years of their manhood, and found in place of them a passion and mastery and exultancy in living that glows to the last twilight of their day: and in the end, when they had come to their strength without it, they had honour in all men's mouths. Saintsbury's five times repeated failure at Oxford to obtain a Fellowship cost him something more than the initial sharpness of humiliation—leisure for an absolute exactness of scholarship, even though it was more than made up for by his depth and range: moreover, a loss that touches mediaevalists more nearly, it cost us his *History of the English Scholastics*. But the losses were outweighed by the gains. He married young: he had Prospero's island of enchanted lawn at the beginning of his life instead of at the end, and all his years were transfigured by it: and he was supremely his own master. No fellowship could have cramped him into a Pattison or a Casaubon: but it might have cost us the absolute Saintsbury. He could hardly have read more than he did: and his reading might not have been so continuously shot through with the richness of living. Ironically enough, when at fifty he accepted the Chair of Rhetoric and English Literature at Edinburgh, it cost us his *History of Wine*. Here again, there is a heavy credit side. The twenty years in Edinburgh are the years of the *opera Maiora*, the *Short History of English Literature*, the editing and part writing of the *Periods of European Literature*, the

History of Criticism, the *History of Prosody*, the *History of English Prose Rhythm*. *The Peace of the Augustans* finished in Edinburgh, his *History of the French Novel*, begun in Edinburgh, finished in Bath, have the mellowness of his Indian summer: and its twilight was lit with the gay lanterns of the *Cellar Book*, and for good discourse, the small but weighty *Trivia* of the three *Scrap Books*.

The world fell in love with them: but the reader who knows these only, knows no more than the surface of his mind. 'Of mighty mould, part hero and part saint of learning, he knew, when time came, how to use harbour, inn, and evening hour: but *after* he had crossed ocean and climbed peak: and it is the traffics, discoveries, and ascents, that count—the vast and austere efforts of his manhood, not the ungirt pastimes and pleasantries of age. Posterity would lose without the *Scrap Books*, yes: but their value is that they are by the historian of Criticism and of Prosody.'[1]

His last will and testament recorded his wish that no biography should be written of him, and no letter published. It was, and even his modesty must have known it, to deny himself a surer immortality than the scholar's, a life in men's minds that would have persisted when his vast learning had become a legend like that of Gerbert or of Scaliger. For as a letter-writer he ranks with Walpole and with Lamb, and his letters are to his graver works as the *Colloquies* of Erasmus to his studies in Lucian and Cicero: quintessential. But the refusal, in an age crazed for personal publicity, is a gesture so characteristic of him that it uplifts the heart. This is the man we knew: not the Johnsonian Saintsbury who loved to fold his legs and have

[1] A. Blythe Webster in the *University of Edinburgh Journal*, 1933.

his talk out: not the Meredithian Saintsbury, emerging from his cellar with a bearded Hermitage reverently and triumphantly bestowed: but the solitary scholar who was his own best company, 'Lord not only of Joyous Gard but also of Garde Douleureuse', reading, reading, reading through the small hours in the familiar chair with the two tall candlesticks behind it. And their light falls, not on his face, but on the open book.

H. W

I
LIFE AND PLAYS

ALL writing which is not of the loosest kind about Shakespeare must, almost necessarily, be dominated by one of two distinct estimates of the positive information available on the subject. There is the view that all this information really comes, as a matter of fact, to very little; and there is the view that, as a matter of fact, it comes to a good deal. The former is the more common, and—though the other has been held by persons whose opinion deserves the utmost respect, and to whom our debt for the labour they have spent on the question is very great—it is probably the sounder. The more impartially, the more patiently and the more respectfully, so far as regards the laws of critical and legal evidence, we examine the results of Halliwell-Phillipps among dead, and of Sidney Lee[1] among living, enquirers, the more convinced do we, in some cases, at least, become that almost the whole matter is 'a great Perhaps', except in two points: that one William Shakespeare of Stratford-on-Avon was, as a man of letters, actually the author of at any rate the great mass of the work which now goes by his name, and that, as a man, he was liked and respected by nearly all who knew him. These things are proved, the first critically, the second legally and historically. To the critical certainties we can add considerably, and to the critical probabilities immensely. But, legally and historically, we are left,

[1] Sir Sidney Lee died in 1926.

at least in the way of certainties, with a series of dates and facts mostly relating to matters of pure business and finance—a skeleton which is itself far from complete, and which, in most points, can only be clothed with the flesh of human and literary interest by the most perilous process of conjecture. We are not quite certain of the identity of Shakespeare's father;[1] we are by no means certain of the identity of his wife; we do not know, save by inference, that Shakespeare and she ever went through the actual ceremony of marriage; we do not know when he began his dramatic career; we know the actual date of the first production of very few of his pieces, let alone that of their composition. Almost all the commonly received stuff of his life story is shreds and patches of tradition, if not positive dream work. We do not know whether he ever went to school. The early journey to London is first heard of a hundred years after date. The deer stealing reason for it is probably twenty years later. The crystallisation of these and other traditions in Rowe's biography took place a hundred and forty-six years after the poet's supposed birth. To hark back: it is not absolutely certain, though it is in the highest degree probable, that the 'Shake-scene' in Greene's

[1] Saintsbury wrote these pages in 1909. At that date Halliwell-Phillipps's *Outlines of the Life of Shakespeare* and Lee's *A Life of William Shakespeare* were the standard works of reference for the facts of Shakespeare's life. Both have been superseded and comprehended in Sir E. K. Chambers's *William Shakespeare: a study of facts and problems*, 1930, which includes much information concerning the family and circumstances of John Shakespeare not available in 1909.

18

outburst is Shakespeare. 'Shake-scene' is not so very much more unlikely a term of abuse for an actor than 'cushion-' or 'tub-thumper' for a minister. And Chettle's supposed apology is absolutely, and, it would seem, studiously, anonymous. The one solid ground on which we can take our stand is supplied by Ben Jonson's famous, but mainly undated, references. They form the main external evidence for the two propositions which have been ventured above; to them, as to a magnetic centre, fly and cling all the contemporary, and shortly subsequent, scraps of evidence that are true metal; they supply the foundation piece on which a structure, built out of internal evidence, may be cautiously, but safely, constructed. Next to them, though in a different kind, comes Meres's *Palladis Tamia* passage in 1598. The publication dates of *Venus and Adonis*, of *Lucrece*, of the *Sonnets*, as well as the fact and date of the purchase of New Place, are tolerably fast-driven piles; the death date is another; the publication of the first folio yet another. We are not, therefore, in a mere whirl of drifting atoms, a wash of conflicting tides; but we may be more exposed to such a whirl or wash than men who like solid ground could desire.

No biography of Shakespeare, therefore, which deserves any confidence, has ever been constructed without a large infusion of the tell-tale words 'apparently', 'probably', 'there can be little doubt'; and no small infusion of the still more tell-tale 'perhaps', 'it would be natural', 'according to what was usual at the time' and so forth. The following summary will give the certain facts, with those which are generally accepted as the most probable, distinguishing the two classes, so far as is possible, without cumbrous saving clauses, but avoiding altogether mere guesswork, unless it has assumed such proportions in ordinary accounts that it cannot be passed by.

The name of Shakespeare appears to have been very common, especially in the west midlands; and there was a William Shakespeare hanged (cf. his namesake's 'Hang-hog is Latin for bacon') as early as 1248, not far from Stratford itself. In the sixteenth century, the name seems to have been particularly common; and there were at least two John Shakespeares who were citizens of the town about the time of the poet's birth. It has, however, been one of the accepted things that his father was a John Shakespeare (son of Richard), who, at one time, was a 'prosperous gentleman'—or, at any rate, a prosperous man of business as woolstapler, fellmonger and so forth, thinking himself gentleman enough to make repeated applications for coat armour, which, at last, were granted. This John Shakespeare married Mary Arden, an heiress of a good yeomanly family, but as to whose connection with a more distinguished one of the same name there remains much room for doubt. The uncertainty of the poet's birthday is one of the best known things about him. He was baptised on 26 April 1564; and probability, reinforced by sentiment, has decided on the 23rd, St George's day, for the earlier initiation. He would seem to have had three brothers and two sisters.[1]

There was a free grammar school at Stratford, to which, as the son of his father, he would have been entitled to admission; and it has been supposed that he went there. Aubrey, who is almost entirely unsupported, even says that he was a schoolmaster himself. The point is only of importance, first in regard to Jonson's famous ascription to him of 'small Latin and less Greek'; secondly, and much more, in relation to the difficulty which has been raised as to a person of no, or little, education having written the plays. The first count matters little—many schoolboys and some schoolmasters have answered to Ben's description. The second matters much—for it seems to be the ground upon which some persons of wit have joined the many of none who are 'Baconians' or at least against 'the Stratforder', as certain anti-Shakespearean Germans call him.

The difficulty comes from a surprising mixture of ignorance and innocence. A lawyer of moderate intelligence and no extraordinary education will get up, on his brief, at a few days' notice, more knowledge of an extremely technical kind than Shakespeare shows on any one point, and will repeat the process in regard to almost any subject. A journalist

[1] The pedigree printed by Chambers (II, xvi) shows that John Shakespeare and Mary Arden had eight children, four boys and four girls (of whom three died young).

of no greater intelligence and education will, at a few hours' or minutes' notice, deceive the very elect in the same way. Omniscience, no doubt, is divine; but *multi*science—especially multiscience a little scratched and admitting through the scratches a sea-coast to Bohemia and knowledge of Aristotle in Ulysses—is quite human. What is wonderful is not what, in the book sense, Shakespeare knew, but what he did and was. And the man—whoever he was—who wrote what Shakespeare wrote would have had not the slightest difficulty in knowing what Shakespeare knew.

The stories of his apprenticeship (to a butcher or otherwise) are, again, late, very uncertain and, in part—such as his making speeches to the calves he was to kill—infinitely childish, even when quite possibly true. The story of his marriage, though starting from some positive and contemporary facts, is a very spider's web of unsubstantial evolution. On 28 November 1582, two husbandmen of Stratford, named Sandells and Richardson, became sureties for £40 in the consistory court of Worcester to free the bishop from liability in case of lawful impediment, by pre-contract or consanguinity, to the marriage of 'William Shagspeare and Anne Hathwey' which might proceed hereupon with only one publication of banns. On 26 May 1583, Shakespeare's eldest daughter, Susanna, was baptised at Stratford. Moreover (a much more surprising thing than this juxtaposition), on the very day before the signing of the bond, a regular licence was issued for the marriage of William Shakespeare and Anne *Whateley*—a coincidence extraordinary in any case, most extraordinary if we note the extreme closeness of the names *Hathwey* and *Whateley* and remember that *Anne* Hathaway is not otherwise traceable, though *Agnes* Hathaway (the two names are in practice confused) is. This mystery, however, has been less dwelt on than the irregular character of the 'bond' marriage and its still more irregular chronological adjustment to the birth of Susanna. On this, on the apparent fact that the wife was eight years older than the husband, who was only eighteen, on his long absences from Stratford and on the solitary bequest (and that an afterthought) of his second-best bed to his wife, have been founded romances, moralisings, censures, defences, hypotheses of formal antenuptial contract, every possible symptomatic extravagance of the *lues commentatoria*, every conceivable excursion and alarum of the hunt after mares' nests. The only rational course of conduct is to decline to solve a problem for which we have no sufficient data; and which, very likely, is no problem at all. Only, as Shakespeare's works have been ransacked for references to disapproval of marriages in which the bride is older than the husband, and to anticipations of marriage privileges, let us once more appeal to the evidence of those works themselves. No writer of any time—and his own time was certainly not one of special respect for marriage—has represented it so constantly as not only 'good' but 'delightful', to retort La Rochefoucauld's injurious distinction. Except Goneril and Regan, who, designedly, are monsters, there is hardly a bad wife in Shakespeare—there are no unloving, few unloved, ones. It is not merely in his objects of courtship—Juliet, Viola, Rosalind, Portia, Miranda—that he is a woman-worshipper. Even Gertrude—a questionable widow—seems not to have been an unsatisfactory wife to Hamlet the elder as she certainly was not to his brother. One might hesitate a little as to Lady Macbeth as a hostess—certainly not as a wife. From the novice sketch of Adriana in the *Errors* to the unmatchable triumph of Imogen, from the buxom honesty of Mistress Ford to the wronged innocence and queenly grace of Hermione, Shakespeare has nothing but the *beau rôle* for wives. And if, in this invariable gynaecolatry, he was actuated by disappointment in his own wife or repentance for his own marriage, he must either have been the best good Christian, or the most pigeon-livered philosopher, or the most cryptic and incomprehensible ironist, that the world has ever seen. Indeed, he might be all these things, and feel nothing of the kind. For the next incident of the biographic legend—the deerstealing and consequent flight to London—there is, it has been said, no real evidence. It is not impossible, though the passage in *The Merry Wives of Windsor* which has been supposed to be a reference to the fact is at least equally likely to be the source of the fiction. That Shakespeare went to London somehow there can be no doubt; how, and when, and for what

24

reason, he went, there can be no certainty. If the Greene reference be accepted, he must have been there long enough to have made a reputation for himself in 1592; by next year, 1593, the year of *Venus and Adonis*, he had begun his unquestionable literary career, and made the acquaintance of Lord Southampton; and, by next year again (1594) (though at the end of it), we first find him a member of the famous company of which he became a leader, and which included Burbage, Heminge, Condell and other persons famous in connection with him.

How long the career—which emerges from obscurity, perhaps with the first, certainly with the second and third of these dates and facts—had been going on is, again, guesswork. Casting back, however, we get a reasonable *terminus ante quem non*, if not a certain *terminus a quo*, in the birth of twins (Hamnet, who died young and Judith, who lived) to him and his wife, before 2 February 1585, when they were baptised. Four years later, again, than 1594, the Meres list of 1598 shows to Shakespeare's name, besides *Venus and Adonis* and *Lucrece* (1594), the goodly list of plays which will be seen presently, and the as yet unprinted *Sonnets*, while Shakespeare had also become at least a competent actor—a business not to be learnt in a day—and had acquired money enough to buy, in 1597, the famous New Place, the largest house in his native town.

The literary progress of these nine or thirteen years, according as we take the first theatrical record or the Meres list for goal, can be assigned, in some cases, with certainty: of the life, hardly anything whatever is known. Legends about horse-holding at theatres, in the first place; of the organisation of a brigade of horse-boys, in the second; of promotion to callboy and to actor—are legends. William Shakespeare's name seems to occur, in April 1587, in a deed relating to some property in which his family were interested. Otherwise, all positive statements in biographies of credit will be found qualified with the 'doubtless' or the 'probably', the 'may have' and the 'would have', until we find him taking part in the Christmas entertainments presented to the queen at Greenwich on St Stephen's day and Innocents' day 1594. Then, and then only, does the mist disappear; though it hardly leaves him in a very lively 'habit as he lived'. But we have mentions of houses in London and (before the New Place purchase) at Stratford; details of financial disaster to his father which seems to have been repaired, and of the subsequent application for arms, in his father's name, which was at last granted in 1596; suits about the property in dispute ten years earlier—a good many business details, in short, but little more that is satisfying.

But the nature of commentators abhors a vacuum: and this vacuum has been filled up (excluding for the present the various arrangements of the *Works*) from two different sides. In the first place, we have a series of conjectures dealing with the progress of Shakespeare's novitiate as actor and playwright, and his relations to his immediate predecessors in the latter capacity. In the second, we have the application of hypothetical hermeneutics to the *Sonnets*.[1]

The first is guesswork pure and unadulterated; or, to speak with more correctness, adulteration without any purity, except in so far as concerns the *Works* themselves—which are reserved for the moment. From them, it derives whatever shadow of substance it possesses. We do not know that Shakespeare ever personally knew a single one of the 'university wits'. The Greene reference, taken at its fullest possible, is, distinctly, against personal knowledge. The Chettle reference, from its obvious and definite disclaimer of personal knowledge, strengthens the counter-evidence. The (probably much later) passages in *The Returne from Pernassus* give no support to it. Parodies of phrasings universal in Elizabethan drama go for practically nothing. And the famous and beautiful appeal to the 'Dead Shepherd' in *As You Like It* contains as little to indicate that, wherever Shakespeare was and whatever he did, from 1585 to 1593, his circle and that of the 'wits' anywhere overlapped.

So, also, the present writer can see no valid evidence of any personal connection with Spenser. 'Our pleasant Willy' has, almost necessarily, been given up: the connection of 'Aetion' with Shakespeare appears to be wholly gratuitous. 'No doubt',

---

[1] For the poetical aspect of these, see the following chapter.

as is pointed out, Shakespeare's company, if he belonged to any before 1594, probably, and, after that, certainly, 'toured in the provinces'; but there is no evidence that he ever was, and no necessity that he ever should have been, in Germany or Scotland or Denmark; nor any reason of either kind why he should have surveyed the battlefields of Towton or of Shrewsbury or of Bosworth any more than those of Actium or Pharsalia. London and Stratford are the only places in which, from evidence, we can place him. Excepting his family, business folk in the two places mentioned, Lord Southampton and Ben Jonson, there are hardly any persons with whom, on evidence, we can associate him.

This manner of handling the subject must, of course, be profoundly unsatisfactory to those who think that, in consequence of the long discussions of biographical facts and fictions by scholars, 'final judgments' should be possible on such points as Shakespeare's marriage, his religious views, his knowledge of law, his conduct in business relations and the like. It seems to be impossible to get a very large number of presumably educated and not un-intelligent people to perceive the difference between proof and opinion. In all the instances just given, we have no basis for proof; and, as to all of them, opinion can never be final, because every person of fair intelligence and education has a right to his own. Of such argument as that Shakespeare's father could not have been a butcher because he was a glover and guild rules forbade the combination, there can be no end. Those who love it may follow it in its endless course; it cannot be too peremptorily asserted that those who do not love it are entitled to reject it entirely and to say 'fight Tradition: fight Presumption' to this shadowy dog and that unsubstantial bear.

The solid fact, however, of Meres's mention of the *Sonnets*, two of which (though the whole collection was not published till ten years later) appeared surreptitiously, it would seem, next year (1599), introduces another range of hypothetical exercise in biography, which has sometimes been followed in opposition to the former method, but has been more frequently combined with it so as to permit of even more luxuriant and wilder expatiation. This is the autobiographic reading of Shakespeare's work; and, more particularly, of the *Sonnets* themselves. The extravagances of this 'method' are a by-word; yet it may be questioned whether almost everybody— sometimes in the very act of protesting against them —has not been caught in the mazy meshes. Are we to say to John Shakespeare 'Thou art *this* man', when we read about testy and platitudinous fathers like old Capulet and Egeus and Polonius? Should we substitute the 'best silver bowl' argument for the 'second-best bed' argument and, calling in *The Tempest*, see Judith Quiney, to whom that bowl was left, in Miranda? Criticism, it is to be feared, shakes its head and observes that the 'colours' of different ages date from long before Aristotle; and that, doubtless, there were charming girls even before Nausicaa.

It may, however, be fully admitted that the *Sonnets* stand in a very different category from that of the plays. Not only does the poet of this kind speak *ex professo* from his heart, while the dramatist speaks *ex professo* as an outside observer and 'representer', but there is no poetry of this kind which approaches Shakespeare's *Sonnets* in apparent vehemence and intensity of feeling. There is even hardly any which mingles, with the expression of that feeling, so many concrete hints, suggesting so broadly a whole romance of personal experience, as they do. How are we to take all this?

One of the best known things in Shakespearean study—even to those who have hardly dabbled in it—is that one of the ways in which it has been taken is an endless series of earnest and almost frantic attempts to reconstruct this romance as a history. The personality of the 'Mr W. H.' to whom the complete edition of 1609 is dedicated, though perhaps the chief, is but one, of the points of dispute. The reality and identity of the fair young man and the dark lady who are by turns or together concerned in the *Sonnets* themselves come next, and, with some enquirers, first; while the incidents and sentiments, expressed, implied, commemorated, in them, have occupied a not small library of discussion, appreciation, attack, defence and so forth.

The extravagance of much of this has always been perceptible to impartial observers; and, perhaps, the extravagance of most of it—except the particular theory to which they are themselves inclined—has been clear enough even to the theorists themselves. Sometimes—and of late with especial learning and elaboration by Sidney Lee—a sort of general *caveat* has been entered on the ground of the peculiarly traditional and conventional character of sonnet writing, especially at this particular time. Sometimes, all attempts to interpret have been shaken off, angrily, contemptuously or critically, according to temperament. And it may be suspected that some people who would confess it, and more who would not, have always inclined to Hallam's curious but courageous wish that Shakespeare 'had never written them'.

But he did write them—there is hardly a thing of his as to the authorship of which—what with Meres's early ascription, the publication with his name seven years before his death and the entire absence of denial, counter-claim, or challenge of any kind—we can be so certain. And, probably, there is no lover of poetry as poetry who would not wish that anything else 'had never been written', so that these might be saved. But, undoubtedly, the mean is very hard to hit in the interpretation of these poems. Although it is quite certain that the sonnet tradition, starting from Petrarch and continued through generations of Italian, French and English practitioners, had resulted in a vast and complicated 'common form' of expression—a huge mass of *publica materies* of which the individual builder took

31

his store, sometimes directly from other individuals, sometimes indirectly—it is possible to lay too much stress on this. After all, even if the sonnet thoughts and phrases were as stereotyped as the figures of a pack of cards—and they were not quite this—there is infinite shuffling possible with a pack of cards, infinite varieties of general game and still more of personal play, above all, infinite varieties of purpose and stake. You may play 'for love' in one sense or 'for love' in another and a very different one. You may play for trifles or for your last penny—to show your skill, or merely to win, or to pass the time, or from many other motives. That Shakespeare was the Deschapelles or Clay of sonnet whist is pretty certain. But that he did not play merely for pastime is almost more so to any one who takes the advice of Sidney's 'Look *in thy heart*' and applies it to reading, not writing.

The *Sonnets*, then, are great poetry, that is to say, in a certain sense, great fiction; and they are intense expressions of feeling, that is to say, in another certain sense, great facts. But to what extent and degree are this fiction and this fact dosed and proportioned? How are we to separate them? How do they colour and react upon one another? Here, no doubt, is the rub—and it is a rub which it seems to the present writer impossible to remove or lubricate. Once more, to those who have accustomed themselves really to weigh evidence, it is impossible to accept it either as proved or disproved that 'Mr W. H.' was Pembroke, or Southampton, or any other friend-patron of Shakespeare, or merely somebody concerned with the publication, or, in fact, a 'personage' of any kind in this play. Nor is it possible to extricate, from the obscurity in which, to all appearance designedly, they were involved, either the other *dramatis personae* or even, save to the vaguest extent, the *scenario* itself. Friendship and love—*bene velle* and *amare*—exchange parts, combine, divorce, sublimate or materialise themselves and each other in too Protean a fashion to be caught and fixed in any form. The least unreasonable of all the extravagant exegeses would be that the whole is a phantasmagoria of love itself, of all its possible transformations, exaltations, agonies, degradations, victories, defeats. The most reasonable explanation, perhaps, and certainly not the least Shakespearean, is that it is partly this—but partly, also, in degree impossible to isolate, a record of actual experience. And it is not unimportant to observe that the *Sonnets*, a lock in themselves, become a key (Dryden would have recognised the catachresis) to the plays. How far they reveal Shakespeare's facts may be doubtful; his method of treating fact, his own or others, is clear in them.

Before generalising on what this is, we may turn to the individual plays themselves, to which we have now come in well grounded chronological advance. The Meres list is well known; it is as follows: *Gentlemen of Verona,* [*Comedy of*] *Errors, Love labors Lost, Love labours wonne, Midsummer night dreame, Merchant of Venice, Richard II, Richard III, Henry IV, King*

John, *Titus Andronicus* and *Romeo and Juliet*. Of these, we know all—for the proposed rejection of *Titus Andronicus* will be dealt with presently—except *Love's Labour's Won*, which has been identified, as plausibly as mere conjecture can identify anything, with *All's Well that Ends Well*. It is, however, all-important to observe that Meres gives no order of sequence; and that so large a bulk of work as this, greater than the whole theatre of some considerable dramatists, must have taken no short time to write, especially when we consider that the writer, during four years unquestionably and, beyond reasonable doubt, for a good deal longer, had been busily employed in acting. Twelve years possibly, since the baptism of Hamnet and Judith, six at least, if we accept the Greene reference, may be suggested as not conjectural items in the problem; eight or ten as a plausible splitting of the difference. To the fruits of this time we may add, fairly enough, if no certainty be insisted upon, Shakespeare's part, whatever it was, in *Henry VI* as well as portions or first sketches of others and, perhaps, some whole plays. But the Meres list, from its solidity, affords such an invaluable basis for investigation and classification that it is wise, in the first place, not to travel outside of it in quest of either external or internal evidence of order, or characteristics of quality.

The external evidence is of the smallest. No one of the plays except *Titus* was published till the year before Meres wrote, and some not till the folio of 1623. The *Comedy of Errors* was acted near the close

34

of 1594. The Greene reference quotes a line of
Henry VI—not a Meres play. Several, *Romeo and
Juliet*, *Richard II*, *Richard III*, were printed in 1597;
Love's Labour's Lost (with alterations) in the next
year. *Titus Andronicus* was acted in January 1593/4
and printed in the latter year, in which *The Merchant
of Venice*, as *The Venetian Comedy*, may have appeared.
This is all; and it will be observed, first, that much
of it comes close up to the Meres date itself; secondly,
that it concerns only a few of the plays. We have,
therefore, to fall back on internal evidence, as it is
called. But internal evidence is of very different
kinds; and it is important to distinguish them from
each other with the greatest possible care. One
kind—or, rather, group of kinds—has figured very
largely, indeed, in Shakespearean study. It is based
on what may be broadly called 'allusions'—
passages in the plays which seem to refer to contem-
poraneous and known events, coincidence of the
general subject of them with such events, or, sometimes, references in other more or less certainly
dated work to them. It cannot be too strongly
asserted, from the point of view of the present survey, that this class of evidence is open to the gravest
suspicion. It ought not, of course, to be judged from
its caricatures, as in the case where the mention of
'pepper' is supposed to be connected with a known
capture of a large cargo of that comforting spice.
But, in almost all cases, it is exceedingly difficult
to be sure that the coincidences are not purely
imaginary. Nor is this the worst part of the matter.

35

Admit that they are not purely imaginary—that the actual cited passages may have had some connection with the actual known events. How are we possibly to be certain that these passages were parts of the play as originally acted, much more as originally written? 'Those who live to please must please to live': the topical insertion or 'gag' is one of the best known features of theatrical composition and is probably as old as Thespis in ancient times or Boileau's imaginary pilgrims in modern. Some of Shakespeare's plays, we know, were not printed till nearly thirty years after they were first acted; it is not impossible that, in some cases, the interval may have been even longer. Even if you can date the passage, it will give you no right whatever to date the play accordingly. If, therefore, this whole class of 'evidence' is not to be ruled out bodily, it must be relegated to the utmost margin—kept strictly in the court of the Gentiles.

The other kind of internal evidence is not itself quite homogeneous, except that it is, or should be, always and entirely concerned with literary matters—with the quality, style, construction, form, character generally, of the work. Even here, there are dangers—and quite as fantastic tricks have been played in this way as in the other. By judging piecemeal, by adopting arbitrary standards of judgment and, above all, by considering, not what Shakespeare wrote but what we should like Shakespeare to have written, or think he ought to have written, it is possible to go as far wrong in this as in any way whatever. In no way, however, is it possible to reach so far and so safely, if due precaution be observed and if there be brought to the enterprise, in the first place, a sufficient study of the whole of Shakespeare's work, and, in the second, a competent knowledge of preceding and contemporary English literature.

The invaluableness of the Meres statement is that it provides us with a trustworthy and far reaching criterion between Shakespeare's earlier and his later work. It is, of course, possible that Meres may not have known of some early pieces or may have omitted them by accident; but in a list already so considerable as his and, as in the case of the *Sonnets*, showing knowledge of a more than merely outside character, it is very improbable that he omitted much that was completed, publicly performed and notoriously Shakespeare's. On the other hand, we have this early body of work 'coted' and named as early. If we can discover any characteristics of the kind least likely to deceive—the characteristics of construction, style, prosody—which differ remarkably as wholes from those of the plays not named, or most of them, this will give us light of the most important and illuminative kind. If we can perceive that, in these same respects, the plays of the early list differ from each other singly or in groups—that there is evidence of the same progress and achievement inside the group as there is between it and plays like *Hamlet, As You Like It, Antony and Cleopatra, Othello*—we may almost know that we are in the

37

right path. And we may branch from it, though with caution and almost with fear and trembling, into comparison of the same kind with immediately preceding or contemporary writers, to obtain additional illustration and illumination.

By the steady carrying out of all these processes—the comparison of the Meres list with the other plays; the comparison of the plays in that list with each other; and the comparison of the work of the Marlowe group, of Lyly and of a few other known or unknown writers—the least hasty or fanciful of critics will probably be induced to mark off from the Meres list of undoubtedly early plays a smaller group of almost undoubtedly earlier and, perhaps, a smaller still of probably earliest. From this last, he will probably be wise in refusing to select an 'earliest of all', because the marks of earliness in them are not quite the same. They are all such as would characterise a genius in its novitiate; but it would be an exceedingly rash person who should undertake to say that, of the various kinds of literary measles which they show, one would be likely to attack the patient sooner than another. The group in question consists, as it seems to the present writer, of three plays, which, to mention them in the un-question-begging order of the folio, are *The Comedy of Errors*, *Love's Labour's Lost* and *Titus Andronicus*. *The Two Gentlemen of Verona*, which, in the same notoriously haphazard order, comes before them all, is, in this order of criticism, very near them as a whole, but with perhaps later qualities; and so is

Meres's probable *Love's Labour's Won* (*All's Well that Ends Well*). Let us take the five in order and the three, together and separately, first. That *The Comedy of Errors* is, in substance, a mere adaptation of the *Menaechmi* of Plautus would, in itself, have very little to do with probable earliness or lateness; for it is a point so well known as to require no discussion, explanation, apology or even frequent statement, that Shakespeare never gave himself the slightest trouble to be 'original'. Its earliness is shown by the comparative absence of character, by the mixed and rough-hewn quality of the prosody (a connected view of Shakespeare's versification will be given later) and, last and most of all, by the inordinate allowance of the poorest, the most irrelevant and, occasionally, the most uncomely word-play and 'foolery'. This last characteristic has, of course, been charged against Shakespeare generally, and the charge will have to be dealt with in general. It need only be said now that in no play or passage from *The Tempest* to *Pericles* is there anything to which, as it seems to the present writer, the words above used can be applied as they can to passage after passage between the Dromios and their masters. He does not therefore think, as would some, that Shakespeare did not write these latter passages; he does think that Shakespeare wrote them before he knew better. But that Shakespeare was certain to know better before long is proved in this very play by the fine, though stiff, tirades of the opening scene, by the extremely beautiful poetry of

Adriana and her sister, as well as by touches of nascent power over character in both of them, and by numerous flashes here and there in which the spirit, not quite full-grown as yet, hurries itself through the bonds of imperfect training in speech and metre. It is, however, on the whole, the crudest and most immature of all the plays, and may well have been the earliest. That position has more commonly been assigned to *Love's Labour's Lost*, and here, too, the assignment has justifications, though they are different. The play exhibits not so much (though there is something of this) the inability of youth to finish, as its prodigality and want of selection. The poet cannot make up his mind what metre to select: blank verse, couplets, stanzas, fourteeners more or less doggerel—he tries them all by turns and does them all with a delightful improvisation. He has a real plot—partly borrowed, of course—but he overloads it in every direction with incident and character. Of the latter, in hasty but astonishingly creative forms, he is the most prodigal of younkers. Nobody is a mere figurehead: Biron, Armado, Holofernes, Costard, Rosaline, even Sir Nathaniel, are of the true Shakespearean family; and the exquisite Shakespearean lyric makes its appearance. There is almost everything in the piece but measure and polish; and one is almost tempted to say: 'Measure and polish are most excellent things; but they can wait or we can wait for them.'

Titus Andronicus, as we have it, has been denied to Shakespeare, but this denial really passes the bounds of all rational literary criticism. The play, we know, was acted and published in 1594; it is included with Shakespeare's by Meres in 1598; it is included in the folio by Shakespeare's intimates and dramatic associates in 1623. If we are to disregard a three-fold cord of evidence like this, the whole process of literary history becomes a mere absurdity—a game of All Fools, with the prize for the craziest topsy-turvyfier, as Thackeray would say, of actual fact. It is, of course, possible—almost everything is possible —that the wrong play got into the folio, that Meres was mistaken, that the piece acted and printed in 1594 was not Shakespeare's; but it is also possible that all the world is mad, except the inhabitants of lunatic asylums. As it happens, too, there are reasons given for the denial; and these reasons are valueless. *Titus* is the one play of Shakespeare which is assuredly of the Marlowe school; the one play, too, which is almost wholly what is called 'repulsive' throughout; the one play in which (see below) the stiff 'single moulded' blank verse line hardly ever—but not never—ruffles itself and grows social. Granted: but this is exactly what we should expect as one very probable result of the novitiate in such a case as Shakespeare's. Considering the shreds and patches in the same style which are actually to be found in his work up to *Macbeth* and *King Lear*, not to say *Hamlet*; considering, further, the genuinely Shakespearean character of Aaron, and the genuinely Shakespearean poetry of more than one or two passages—the internal evidence would be strong. Joined to the external, it is simply irresistible. But the novitiate on another side is equally unmistakable here: though the novice, scholar, tiro, explorer (call him what you will) is in a different mood. He is playing a particular game—the game of the tragedy with horror as its main motive and a stately, but monotonous and verbally 'bombasted', blank verse as its vehicle. In a certain sense, it is the complement of *The Comedy of Errors* and might be called *The Tragedy of Horrors*—outrage and bloodshed taking the place of horseplay and buffoonery for stuff, rhetorical and conceited diction that of wordplay and coarseness for language. And, as there, so here, the novice, though he cannot keep his identity and quality wholly invisible, cramps and curbs them in order to play somebody else's game. In the order of thought, perhaps, *Love's Labour's Lost* should come later—as a burst of relief, an incoherent but untrammelled exercise in the writer's own game or games for his own pleasure. But even a Shakespeare is unlikely to write two plays like *Love's Labour's Lost*; or, rather, a Shakespeare is least likely of all men to write them. He will do better or worse, accordingly as he pays more or less attention to parts of his composition, while improving that composition itself. He will have more of the picture and less of the panorama or kaleidoscope; but it does not follow that his whole picture will, for a time at least, have as much charm.

And this is the state of things that we actually find in *The Two Gentlemen of Verona* and *All's Well that*

Ends Well. Julia, in the former, as a serious character, and Parolles, in the latter, as a comic personage, are much above anything that Shakespeare had hitherto done in the way of live human figures. The plot, though 'romantic' enough in both, is much closer knit and more thoroughly carried out by the *dramatis personae* than the shuffle of stock characters in the *Errors*, the sanguinary dream procession of *Titus*, or the masque-like intricacies of *Love's Labour's Lost*. The verse, still of the same general character, is settling down towards blank verse only and that blank verse free. But the progress is not like that of a faultless and hopeless schoolboy, who proceeds with even excellence from one class to another. There are relapses, as, at least, in part (not all) of the business of Launce and his dog, in *The Two Gentlemen*; there are failures to advance or even thoroughly to 'know where he is', as in that part of Helena which has been very differently judged. It does not matter very much whether those are right who consider her a touching example of a wronged and loving woman, conquering through constancy and wisdom, or those who think her 'Shakespeare's only disagreeable heroine'—one who makes confusion of marriage and something very different, who practically swindles a man into indissoluble connection with her, and who, in short, when we contrast her, say, with Cleopatra, is the more really vicious of the pair. Either view may be right; but, if this play were of a later date, Shakespeare would have taken more care to prevent

43

the uncertainty—or would, at any rate, have left the worse interpretation on the shoulders of the interpreters, as he has done in the case of Ophelia. Still, there are great things in both these plays, though, emphatically, they are experiments still, and experiments in which the ill success is more conspicuous from the very fact that they aim higher. The poetical beauties in *The Two Gentlemen* are, occasionally, of all but the very highest kind, while in *All's Well* there is much fine verse, Lafeu is a comic, not burlesque, character of great interest, and there is a further advance towards the Shakespearean clown proper.

There is, however, another candidate for the *alias* of *Love's Labour's Won* which seems to have much less claim to it, but which, undoubtedly, is early—in fact, in all probability, one of Shakespeare's earliest adaptations of other men's work. This is the popular, and, in parts, very amusing, but only in parts original, *Taming of the Shrew*. A play entitled *The Taming of a Shrew* appeared in 1594, and, from this, the Shakespearean piece is adapted, with not a little of 'his own sauce', as Mrs Tibbs would say, in the main or Petruchio portion, an addition in the shape of the doubly contrasted sister Bianca, and some very curious local allusions (in the induction) to Shakespeare's own country. The Bianca part of the subject had been taken from the Italian much earlier by Gascoigne. The story was sure to catch the public taste, and the play was actually taken up long afterwards by Fletcher for the purpose of reversing it and

44

showing 'the tamer tamed'. The situations, though in the farcical division of comedy, are of general appeal, and Shakespeare has made the very utmost of them—indeed, there are few more remarkable instances of his power of transforming marionettes into men and women than Petruchio and Katharine. But much of the verse, even in the added portions, is of quite early 'university wit' character—singly-moulded lines, the trick of repetition of the speaker's own name instead of 'I', 'my', and so forth, Latin tags and the like. Indeed, some have questioned whether this part of the addition is Shakespeare's at all. In any case, what is his cannot be late; and, as the original play appears not to be older than 1594, the rehandling, if it be rehandling, must have followed very quickly. And there is very little to say for the identification with *Love's Labour's Won*. Petruchio's is an odd 'labour of love', and Lucentio seems to be a rather doubtful winner.

As to the other seven named plays in the Meres list, there are practically no means of certain chronological arrangement. Those who choose to do so may, of course, observe that, in *Romeo and Juliet*, the nurse says ''Tis since the earthquake now eleven years', discover that there was an earthquake in 1580 and point to 1591. There was, doubtless, also salmons caught in both years. So, also, in dealing with *The Merchant of Venice*, it has been observed that the queen's physician, Lopez, of Jewish descent, was tried and executed in 1594. And there is an *o* in Lopez and an *o* in Shylock; likewise an *l* in both.

There were marriages in 1595, and there are marriages in *A Midsummer Night's Dream*. Let these things appeal to those to whom they do appeal. Others, perhaps, more happily, may be content to abide by Meres and 'before 1598', except in so far as—without positiveness but making suggestions for what they may be worth—they rely on the kind of internal evidence already outlined. For reasons of convenience, we may take the three plays just mentioned first, leaving the histories for the moment.

For all reasons, *Romeo and Juliet* seems likely to be the earliest. It has not, indeed, quite such a mixture of metres as *A Midsummer Night's Dream* has, and the mere 'picture of young love' may easily deceive us. But, on the other hand, there is much of Marlowe's 'single-moulded' line; and, together with many things among the most magnificent in Shakespeare, there are crudities and inequalities of the kind natural to a beginner. On the other hand, such a beginner as this is not frequent in literature; and he is already far, in more than one or two respects, from his beginnings. Already, we have seen something of that astonishing power of vivification which distinguishes him from all his predecessors; already, the characters have begun to take the play into their own hands, as it were, and to work it out, not regardless of the story, by any means, but in a way that gives to that story a tenfold power and interest. But it has been only in touches—the whole story has never been treated in this way, still less have all the characters undergone this peculiar transforming influence. In *Romeo and Juliet*, much further advance has been made. As before—as always—Shakespeare takes a given story and does not vary the mere incidents much, or add very much to them. But the personages become persons; and this personality extends throughout the drama. Independently of Romeo and Juliet themselves—the very opposites and contradictions of the stock hero and the stock heroine—of Mercutio and the nurse, the whole houses of Montague and Capulet almost down to Antony and Potpan, are alive. There is hardly a figure in the play, except, perhaps, the unfortunate count Paris, to whom Shakespeare has not communicated this vivacity: and Paris had to be a contrast to Romeo. Here, too, not for the first time— for we have seen it in *Love's Labour's Lost*, in *The Two Gentlemen* and even in *Titus Andronicus*—but in far larger measure and intenser form, is the splendid poetry which Shakespeare puts at the service of the drama, as (save in a few flashes of Marlowe and Peele) it had not been put since the great days of Greek tragedy.

There is hardly less of this in *A Midsummer Night's Dream*; though, as comports with comedy, it is of a less poignant and transporting nature. And this play, as was remarked above, is more of an olio of metres. But, in certain respects, it still marks progress. If not in all parts, in the whole, it is the most original of Shakespeare's plays in point of subject up to this time; in fact, it is one of the most original of all in that respect. And this subject is worked up

47

into action with a skill not yet displayed—indeed, Shakespeare here depends more on incident than on character. It is not always fully recognised how artfully the several motives—the Theseus and Hippolyta story, the quarrel of Oberon and Titania, the fortunes of the lovers and the 'tedious brief play'— work into each other and work out each other. Popular as fairy mythology had, in a manner, been, nobody had made anything like this use of it; it is only necessary to name Gloriana and Titania, in order to prove any *rapprochement* of Spenser and Shakespeare on this head to be out of the question. Puck 'was feared in field and town' long before Shakespeare; but Shakespeare's Puck is something very different from a mere 'lob of spirits'. The multiplicity of the interests and beauties in this short play is almost bewildering: there is the stuff of half a dozen poetical comedies in it, yet not in the least confusedly disposed.

The Merchant of Venice presents a somewhat different problem. Here, also, there are many actions: nor, perhaps, are they much less well connected than those of the *Dream*, though they lack the subtle excuse for rapid and interfluent metamorphosis which the very title 'A Midsummer Night's' *Dream* supplies in the other case. There need be no cavilling on this score—in fact, on the 'relief' system, the system of tragic and comic interchange and conflict which makes English drama, the chequers are even better placed. The plot of Shylock against Antonio, the casket scenes, the trial and the trick on the

48

husbands, with the Lorenzo and Jessica 'trace-horse' or 'outrigger' interest, provide a vivid wave-like change of intensity and relief, which even the fierce vexation of Puck's persecution of the mid-summer lovers does not give. But, from another point of view, the *Merchant* is less mature than the *Dream*; or, rather, some of its parts are. The Morocco and Arragon sections, at least, of the casket scenes are quite of the Marlowe period in verse, and, to some extent, in handling; the bantering of the lovers behind their backs, part of the Gobbo business and other things belong to the unripe clowning which is at its greenest in the *Errors* and has ripened con-summately in, say, *As You Like It*. On the other hand, the trial is admittedly among the *apices* of dramatic poetry; and the whole characters of Shy-lock and Portia are among the *dramatis personae* of eternity. To the present writer, it has for many years been a moral certainty that these different parts are of different dates, and that a similar difference pre-vails much more largely in Shakespeare's work than is sometimes thought. The single-plot drama, with its beginning, middle and end, could, perhaps, not easily be written in this way. But the drama which, though not patchwork, is interwoven, can be thus written.

The chronicle plays, *King John, Richard II* and *III* and *Henry IV*, which are certainly early because mentioned by Meres, introduce a new division of Shakespeare's work, to which we shall take the liberty of adding *Henry VI pro tanto*. In the opinion of the present writer, the *tantum* is considerable. In

the case of all these plays, with the possible exception of *Richard II* (both the *Richards* were actually
published in 1597), there were previously existing
pieces on the subject; whether in all cases these
were the actual pieces that we have is another
question. But in no kind of drama would the
specially Shakespearean method find better exercise
than in the chronicle history. That remarkable
species, though it was to receive its perfect development only in England, and (in absolute perfection)
only at the hands of Shakespeare himself, had, as has
been seen, made its appearance as a modernised
and practicalised development of the mystery and
morality, much earlier in the sixteenth century. The
advantages of the species, when it discards allegory
altogether and at least affects to be frankly historical,
are obvious: subjects that 'come home', copiousness
and variety of interest, given outlines of striking
figures, and the like. Its dangers—hardly less
obvious—are those of the prosaic and the promiscuous; of a mere decoction of chronicle facts and
speeches, fortified by bombast and frothed with
stock horseplay. And these are abundantly exem-
plified in the earliest Elizabethan specimens, while
they are by no means absent from the curious later
attempts of Dekker, Middleton and others to combine a more or less historical mainplot with a purely
fictitious underplot, romantic or classical. Now,
Shakespeare's two greatest gifts, that of sheer poetic
expression and that of character creation, were
exactly what was needed to turn these 'formless

agglomerations' into real organisms, possessing life and beauty. If *Richard II* be quite original (which, as has been hinted, it would not be wise to assume too absolutely) it must be a good deal earlier than its publication, but later than *Titus Andronicus*, with which, however, it may be classed as exhibiting the Marlowe influence more strongly than anything else, save some parts of *Henry VI*, which one would be inclined to place between them. In yet other respects, *Richard II* makes a very fair pair with *Romeo and Juliet* in its far different division. The curious immature splendour of the conception of the title part is like nothing else in Shakespeare. The parallel with, and the suggestion given by, Marlowe's *Edward II* are, of course, unmistakable. But, where Marlowe has given three Edwards, not perhaps irreconcilable with each other but not actually reconciled, Shakespeare's Richard *sibi constat* throughout, in weakness as in strength—he is sincere in his insincerity. Still, the part is not well supported— even of 'time-honoured Lancaster' it may be said that he rather makes great speeches than is a great character; and so of others. The chronicle sequence, encroaching rather on dramatic connection, is also noticeable; as is the fact (especially to be considered in view of *Titus Andronicus* and Marlowe) that there is practically no comic element whatever. Of the extreme beauty of the poetry (almost always, however, of the 'purple patch' or 'fringe' kind and, it would seem, purposely so) in the king's part, it is almost unnecessary to speak.

51

King John and *Richard III*, on the other hand, are examples—documented, as we may say, and almost acknowledged—of adaptation, of the working up of existing materials. But not many impartial and competent critics will adopt Greene's very unkind simile of the crow and the feathers. It is much rather a case of grafting the fairest and most luscious fruit on a crab-tree or a sloe, though no metaphor of the kind can be satisfactory. The processes and results of the adaptation, however, are rather different in the two cases. In *King John*, Shakespeare took and kept more of the original; but he heightened the presentation incomparably. The famous part of Constance is almost wholly his own; he has done much to the king, not a little to the bastard, hardly less to Arthur and Hubert. Above all, he has (to quote an absurd boast of another person a century later) 'made it a play'—a piece of life and not a sample of chronicling. Hardly anywhere will the student find better examples of Shakespeare's craftsmanship in verse and phrase—of the way in which, by slightly adding, cancelling, smoothing, inspiriting, he turns a lame line or passage into a beautiful one —than in *King John*, compared with its original.

Richard III, on the other hand, bears very much less resemblance to its predecessor, *The True Tragedie of Richard III*, and some have regarded it as almost an independent following of Marlowe's *Edward II*. It certainly resembles that play in bursts of poetry of a somewhat rhetorical kind, in the absence of purely comic episodes or scenes and in the concentration of character interest on the hero. Not quite, however, in this latter point. For the character of Margaret (which seems to the present writer to be definitely connected with the Angevin princess's part in *Henry VI*, and Shakespearean throughout) is greater than any secondary part in *Edward II*. *Richard III*, too, in the famous wooing scene, has a scene of character, as distinguished from a mere display of it, which is unmatched elsewhere. And, perhaps, as a whole, the play has been too much and too commonly regarded as a mere melodrama or popular blood-and-thunder piece, with Clarence's dream and some other *placebos* thrown in. It is, at any rate, full of life—with nothing in it either of the peculiar dream quality of Marlowe or of the woodenness of certain other early playwrights.

As was above observed, the part due to Shakespeare in *Henry VI* cannot be minutely discussed here. It seems to the present writer to be probably large. There is, at least, no doubt that many of the passages which it used to be the fashion to dole out to the university wits, like beef bones at a buttery door in ancient days, are quite like those in Shakespeare's plays of the period which we have already surveyed. And it may seem to some that many scenes—some of them, no doubt, not wholly or originally from his pen—many of the battle pieces, French and English; the starting of the rose dispute; the quarrel of Winchester and Gloucester and the deaths of both; all, as has been said, of the scenes where Margaret appears; much of the Cade part;

the deaths, again, of York and Clifford; of prince
Edward and king Henry—smack of Shakespeare in
their altered forms. But it would be altogether uncritical to be positive here. It may be sufficient to
say that *Part I* exhibits least change; *Part II* most;
and *Part III* somewhat less than *Part II*, but still a
very considerable amount; while, independently of
positive changes, the whole composition of *Part I*
is very much less Shakespearean, even as compared
with his earliest probable work, than that of the
other two. At any rate, we may safely return to the
position that, in this chronicle work, Shakespeare
had new and admirable opportunities for developing his grasp of character and for getting into complete working order that remarkable and, in fact,
unique, conception of the loose, many-centred drama
kept together by character itself, which was to be
his—and ours.

Last of the Meres-warranted batch comes *Henry
IV*, like the others worked up from an earlier production, *The Famous Victories of Henry the fifth*, but
more remarkable than any of them, if not for passages of pure poetry (for which its theme gives but
rare opportunity), for complete transformation of
the merest brute material into magnificent art. The
first assignment of the world-famous part of Falstaff
—one of the very greatest of dramatic creations, and
practically a creation, in the precise sense of the
word—to the luckless Lollard Oldcastle was a mis-
take; but it was speedily rectified—though not without further protest on the part of the prosaic in

favour of the historical warrior Fastolf. The actual play (for its two parts are practically one) is, undoubtedly, with the reservation above stated, one of Shakespeare's very greatest achievements; and, seeing that he had already proved himself able to supply pure poetry in unlimited quantities and in any required degree of strength, no drawback or shortcoming could possibly be urged. The entwining and enforcing of the purely historical part receives, and, probably, has always received, less attention from readers and spectators; but it is wonderful in itself. The prince (the famous key-soliloquy, 'I know you all' and the other on the crown excepted) is designedly kept undeveloped in his public capacity. But the king, the Percies, Glendower, the younger princes and wiser noblemen, are all vivified and spirited up in the inscrutable Shakespearean manner. Still, 'the general' are not wrong in preferring to dwell on the Bohemian society of which the prince is the rather Mephistophelian centre, but of which Falstaff is the real master and king. Not a member of it, male or female, but has the certain, vital touches. 'Bowdlerising' is seldom less justified of its works than when it here prevents readers from appreciating the curious and universal humanity of Shakespeare's portraiture, and its contrast with the artificial efforts of modern realism. The supremacy of Falstaff does not disparage the exemplary virtue of Pistol or the modest adequacy of Bardolph and of Nym; and, in the same way, Nell and Doll make each the other *deformitate formosam videri*. Everyone

55

has noticed how, in this most genial, if not most poetical, of his cycles (anticipating, for a moment, *The Merry Wives*), Shakespeare has been prodigal of home memories—of Warwickshire and Gloucestershire detail. But everybody, perhaps, has not noticed the singular fashion in which, once more, this yoking of almost domestic minutiae with public affairs passes itself off, in contrast with the strident discord of *Poetaster* and *The Mayor of Quinborough*. Shallow, immortal in his own way, is a planet in a greater system only; and all the parts combine to work this out.

We are now deprived of the safe, if not in all ways definite, assistance of Meres in respect of chronology; and, for the rest of the contents of the folio as well as for *Pericles* (the single play outside of it which will be considered in the present chapter) we have, in a majority of cases, nothing but guesswork to guide us. But, using the same general principles as heretofore —the internal evidence of versification and dramatic craftsmanship, with such positive aids as may bear investigation, we can continue this history of Shakespeare's work on the same general lines. Only, it will be desirable to adhere to the usual folio order with one single exception, that of *The Tempest*, which, in accordance with general practice (to be critically examined later), we shall keep to the end, putting *Pericles*, which has no folio order, in its place, though by no means asserting that it certainly deserves priority over all the others.

That the whole of *Pericles* is not Shakespeare's is

extremely probable; but the allocation of parts to other dramatists, named or unnamed, is as hazardous a piece of 'hariolation' as has been tried even in this hazardous game. It is not too much to say that there is no part which might not be his; the very choruses which have been denied him are extremely Shakespearean, and group excellently with similar things in *A Midsummer Night's Dream* and *As You Like It*. The brothel scenes can be similarly, if not so completely, paired with passages in the *Errors* and in *Measure for Measure*; and divers examples of stiff Marlowe verse and handling with others in *Titus Andronicus* and the early chronicles and elsewhere. On the other hand, some of the best things throughout the play are *aut Shakespeare aut Diabolus*, and it must have been a most superior fiend who forged the shipwreck passage. Still, nothing is heard of the play till 1608, when it was licensed; and it is pretty certain that, whether the whole was written by Shakespeare or not, the whole was not written by Shakespeare at or near that time. The present writer would be prepared to take either side on the question: 'Did Shakespeare about this time complete an early immature sketch of his own; or did he furnish, voluntarily or involuntarily, scenes to one which was vamped up and botched off by another or others?' But he rather inclines to the first alternative, because of the distinct similarity of the phenomena to those shown in others of Shakespeare's plays actually contained in the folio. That the scheme of the play is not of a mature period is shown by the fact that it has little character, and that what it has is still less concerned with the working out of the action. The contrast here, not merely with *A Winter's Tale* but with the much abused *Cymbeline*, is remarkable.

To cast back to the earlier, but not yet discussed, plays of the canon, *The Merry Wives of Windsor*, as most people know, is a play with a legend—that the queen wished to see Falstaff 'in love', and that it was written in fourteen days to please her. This, however (the later part of which is one of the curious Shakespeare-Molière coincidences), comes only from Dennis, a hundred years after date. The play was actually licensed in 1602, and imperfectly printed next year—dates which suit well enough with the inclusion of *Henry IV* in the Meres list of 1598 and its completion by *Henry V* in that year or 1599. With his usual preference of artistic convenience to prosaic exactitude, Shakespeare has not troubled himself about niching this episode very carefully in his precedent history of the fat knight. Shallow appears duly, but Slender replaces Silence; 'the wild prince and Poins' are referred to, but vaguely. You neither need, nor are you intended, to make a 'harmony' of the four pieces. So, too, it seems to be lost labour and idle sentimentality to lament the decadence and defeat of Falstaff. Men are generally decadent, and frequently defeated, when dealing with women in such circumstances; and Falstaff's overthrow does not make him fall very hard after all. On the other hand, the *vis comica* of the piece is perfect; its exuberant invention and variety are unsurpassed; and the actual construction is more careful than usual. In character and dialogue, it is not surpassed by the very greatest of the plays, allowance being made for kind and atmosphere. Everybody is alive and everything is vividly illuminated—not with the extra-natural, if not non-natural, Congreve rockets, but with a lambent easy light of air. Sir Hugh Evans must have been meant as a brother in dramatic arms to Fluellen, and it is difficult to prefer Roland to Oliver or *vice versa*. The attractive grace—though given in outline merely—of sweet Anne Page is masterly; and, in her mother and Mistress Ford, Shakespeare has given, as hardly another writer has ever succeeded in doing, in *bourgeois* condition and deliberately prosaised tone, the same high but perfectly human standard of wifeliness which, elsewhere, he has carried to the court of poetical quintessence in Hermione and in Imogen. There are few things more amusing to a liberally catholic student of literature than the half patronising, half apologetic, tone adopted, sometimes, towards *The Merry Wives*, as a 'farce'. And, here again, one is reminded of Molière.

Measure for Measure is a more difficult play—one not so liable to be undervalued from inability to perceive that a comic microcosm may be thoroughly cosmic, but more apt to disconcert, if not actually to disgust, by reason of its singular apparent discords, its unusual scheme of conduct and character and its scant reconcilableness with that un-puritan, but fairly severe, system of poetical justice which Shake-

59

speare generally maintains. Its 'disagreeableness' —to use a word often laughed at but expressive and without a synonym—is less to some tastes than that of *All's Well that Ends Well*; but, to a certain extent, it exists. On the other hand, its power is unquestionable, and it contains some of the greatest things in Shakespeare. It was certainly (or almost certainly) performed in 1604, and it has been customary to accept that year as the approximate date of the composition. To the present writer, this seems very improbable, and he would select *Measure for Measure* as the strongest instance of the suggested earliness, in a more or less incomplete form, of many more plays than are contained in Meres's list. Shakespeare, indeed, has improved immensely on the original Italian story and on Whetstone's two English versions, in novel and drama. He has not only added the magnificent scenes between Isabella and Angelo, and Isabella and her brother, and the character (dramatically important, inasmuch as it helps to save Isabella and provides a *dénouement*) of 'Mariana in the moated grange'; he has lavished his nepenthe of poetry on a not particularly attractive theme. But, in the first place, it seems very unlikely that he would have chosen that theme so late; and, in the second, it is nearly certain that, if he had, he would have worked it up with different results. His seventeenth-century plays generally contain nothing so crude as the cruder parts of *Measure for Measure*, while these are very like parts of the early certainties and of *Pericles*. Moreover, even if Pompey and Lucio

were cleaner-mouthed, they would still be un-
finished studies, companions of Launce and Launce-
lot, not of Touchstone and Feste. The play, as a
whole, gives one the idea of an early, half-finished
piece which the writer has resumed, which he has
improved immensely, but on which he has rather
hung additional and separate jewels than spent the
full labour of thorough refashioning and refounding.
Had it come straight from the hands of the Shakespeare of 1604, we should surely have had a much
more defensible and, in fact, intelligible duke, than
the person who runs his state and his servants into
difficulties in order that he may come to the rescue
as a rather shabby Providence—an Angelo more of
a piece, less improbably repentant (not to say so
improbably flagitious) and less flagrantly 'let off'.
If one cared to conjecture, it might be possible to
show a strong case for an original intention to adopt
the story in its blackest shape, *Titus* fashion; a disgust with this leading to the abandonment of the
thing for a time; an inspiration to create a 'Saint
Isabel' and a consequent adaptation and transformation to 'happy ending' and poetical injustice.
But even a Shakespeare cannot reshape ends in a
manner entirely contrary to their rough-hewing,
without some loss of accomplishment, verisimilitude
and effect.

Measure for Measure was never printed in Shakespeare's lifetime; *Much Ado about Nothing*, which
(with the much earlier *Errors* between them) follows
it in the folio and which, like it, is founded on an

Italian story, had been actually printed four years before the alleged date of *Measure for Measure* and is thought to have been written even a year earlier than this. Here, there is neither necessity nor probability for any theory of partial composition. The play is all of a piece; and the best things in it are entirely original. The trick played on Hero had appeared both in Bandello's prose and in Ariosto's verse; and there seems actually to have been an English play on the subject so early as 1583. But Shakespeare added Benedick and Beatrice; he added Dogberry and Verges and he made the whole thing into one of the most remarkable instances of the kind of tragicomedy where no actual tragedy is permitted, but where it is only just avoided, and where tragic motives are allowed to work freely. The play is of extraordinary merit, and Shakespeare has only left one loose stitch—a stitch which he might have picked up with very little trouble—in the entirely unexplained, and very nearly inexplicable, behaviour of Margaret, who, being certainly not a traitress and as certainly not a fool, first lends herself to a proceeding obviously prejudicial to her mistress, and then holds her tongue about it. Except in this point, the play works with perfect ease of action; and, if one does not envy Hero her husband, and does grudge her very much to him, that is no uncommon case. As for Benedick and Beatrice, they are, perhaps, as good touchstones as any in Shakespeare. No one but an 'innocent' can possibly fail to like them; no one but a charlatan will ever pretend not to do so.

The authorities of Messina are more 'farcical'; but the farce, again, is superfarcical.

It might well have been thought that nothing better in the way of romantic comedy would be written. But this was to be triumphantly contradicted by two plays, *As You Like It* and *Twelfth Night*, which are believed to have followed *Much Ado* very quickly, and which, in the folio (with plays already mentioned intervening), observe the order in which they have been named. But it is not positively known which appeared first. *Twelfth Night* was acted on 2 February 1601/2; *As You Like It*, on less certain grounds, is put some two years before. So far as one can judge from internal evidence, *Twelfth Night* would seem to be a little the earlier, or, at any rate, to retain a little more of the characteristics of Shakespeare's earliest comedies. But, in reality, *Much Ado About Nothing, As You Like It* and *Twelfth Night* form a trio of which the best thing to say is that only the man who wrote the other two could have written any one of them. Still, *As You Like It* has a certain pre-eminence, and may put in a claim to be the greatest of Shakespeare's comedies—the typical romantic comedy—excluding *The Tempest* as belonging rather to that middle kind for which there is no English name, but which is inexactly designated *drame* in French. There is hardly more than one fault in it—a fault which, oddly enough, is very rare in Shakespeare, though extremely common in his contemporaries—the fault of concluding the play with a violent 'revolution' merely communicated by a messenger. That an 'old religious man' of Shakespeare's creation might have converted even such an exceedingly unpromising subject as duke Frederick need not be denied: it is very difficult to say what any one of Shakespeare's creation might not have done. But it would have been very interesting to hear the arguments used on the occasion. With this exception, there is nothing that exceeds the licence of romantic character comedy. That was the way they lived in Arden—there can be no doubt of it. And the other things had to happen in order that they might so live. A fresh qualm, succeeded by a fresh desire, may, indeed, be aroused by the announced intention of Jaques to seek duke Frederick's company: the qualm as to his probable reception, the desire to have Shakespeare's account of it. But Jaques himself, with whom some have quarrelled, is a perfectly allowable, and a perfectly admirable, foil to the lovers and the fleeters of the time. The vividness of almost every scene and passage is unmatched even in Shakespeare; there are no *longueurs*; and, if there were, Rosalind and Touchstone would save them. The poet has not here, as he did earlier in *A Midsummer Night's Dream*, and, later, in *The Tempest*, resorted to supernatural machinery to help his glamour. We are no further from ordinary life than romance always is, and in the least extraordinary regions of romance itself. But 'Arden' is none the less made an enchanted ground without spells or incantations, an earthly Paradise, with nothing that is not within reach of

64

almost any human being. Wit, wisdom and poetry are the only transfigurers. Shakespeare, of course, had certainly for canvas Lodge's Euphuist romance of *Rosalynde*; perhaps (it would be pleasant to think so) the *Tale of Gamelyn* itself—but it was merely canvas. The charm of Rosalind, the marrowy moralising of Jaques, the unfailing fool-wisdom of Touchstone, are all his own. By this time, too, he had arrived at that complete command of verse of which something will be specially said later, and had perfected his wonderful prose. Both the blank verse and the lyric in *As You Like It* are in absolute perfection, each for its special purpose; and there is, perhaps, no play (for *Hamlet* lacks the lyric) in which all three media are so perfectly displayed.

As You Like It, with Rosalind as Ganymede, had taken advantage of that habit of representing women's parts by boys which has been supposed to possess advantages in itself. Cleopatra, played by a boy (as with true Shakespearean audacity she is herself made to suggest) must have been absurd, but Shakespeare could not help himself and the custom of the country. Here, he could help himself; and he did so with admirable success. Moreover, the success could evidently be repeated (if the artist were strong enough) in a different key. The artist was strong enough and he repeated it in Viola; relying here on the custom to emphasise and make probable the confusion of brother and sister. *Twelfth Night or What You Will*—the latter title an obvious pendant to *As You Like It*; the former, perhaps unnecessarily, supposed to refer to the time of production—is the purest comedy of all Shakespeare's plays. We know that the captain is in no danger; none, even apparently, threatens any one else. To make Malvolio, as has sometimes been attempted, an almost tragic personage, virtuous and deeply wronged, is an absurdity. The duke is, and is meant to be, a feeble person; but he can talk exquisite poetry, is a gentleman, probably made exactly the sort of husband that Viola wanted and so is one of those subtlest, because most faintly nuanced, criticisms of life which only the greatest masters dare to allow themselves. Feste is not Touchstone's equal—but who is? and, besides, it would not have done for the clown to be wittier than the knight when both were witty—in *As You Like It* things are different. The rest are of the Upper House almost without an exception. Viola, no Rosalind or Beatrice, but a jewel of the other type and differenced exquisitely from such sisters as Juliet and Miranda; Olivia, stately, but perfectly human; Maria, not elaborately, but sufficiently, drawn in the other vein for contrast—form an extraordinary triad even for Shakespeare; and it is afflicting that some commentators should forget that 'the youngest wren of nine' was no 'waiting maid' in the modern sense. On the other side, Sir Toby Belch is one of those doubles that are no doubles, over which nearly all artists stumble. He is of the same genus as Falstaff, but of a different species; and almost entirely different as an individual; just as Sir Andrew is of the tribe of Silence

66

and Slender, but quite other than they. As for Malvolio, he has no parallel anywhere save Molière's Alceste, who, like him but more commonly, has been travestied into a *persona tragica* by incompetent criticism. A gentleman, a man of honour and of his duty, of parts and of merit, his comic ἁμαρτία is compounded of vanity, sourness of temper, lack of humour, a little jack-in-officeship, much ambition and, probably, not a little downright jealousy—and it brings the comic punishment upon him most completely and condignly. Sebastian, no doubt, has extraordinary, but not impossible, luck.

From this point, we may take a liberty—of which we have already given warning—with the folio arrangement. *The Winter's Tale* would come next, according to the division of 'Comedies, Histories and Tragedies', and several histories, earlier according to the Meres *point de repère*, would come next after that. But, according to that class of internal evidence which we have allowed, *The Winter's Tale* is distinctly later; some more plays regarded as 'histories' in Shakespeare's time are, not merely to us, but essentially, romantic tragedies; and the arrangement, according to logic and literature must, in other ways, be altered. We shall rearrange the scene from this point, therefore, recording all certain, or even probable, data as to individual plays as they arise, under four heads—the remaining English histories, the classical plays subsequent to *Titus Andronicus*, the romantic tragedies and the three final *drames*.

The first of the histories is *Henry V*, which was partly drawn from the same originals as *Henry IV*, and followed it closely. It was published (imperfectly) and 'stayed' in 1600; and is supposed to have been acted the year before. The magnificent death of Falstaff almost necessitated the previous turning upon him of the king, which, indeed, had been foreshadowed in *Henry IV*. Partly this, and partly other things, have prejudiced some critics against this 'patriot king', who, nevertheless, is one of the greatest, if not the most attractive, of Shakespeare's creations. The fresh presentment of Pistol and the addition of Fluellen demonstrate the inexhaustibleness of the poet's comic *prosopopoeia*, and, besides the fine tirades which figure in all the extract books, there are innumerable passages of literary excellence. But, in a panoramic survey of Shakespeare's plays, *Henry V*, perhaps, with one exception to be dealt with presently, stands forth most conspicuously as almost the deftest of his spiritings up of chronicles —as a pattern of the difficult accomplishment of vitalising chronicle by character. Here, it is by character diffuse rather than compact—by the extraordinary vivacity of the different personages rather than by interest concentrated in a hero. So far as he is concerned, it is the triumph of Henry of England, rather than that of Harry of Monmouth, in which we rejoice.

The last remaining, and, probably, the last written, of the English group, *Henry VIII*, presents remarkable peculiarities; and it has been usual to take it as Shakespeare's only in parts—Fletcher's, and, perhaps, Massinger's, in others. A play on Henry VIII was represented in 1613 and interrupted by the burning of the playhouse. The piece which, ten years later, appeared in the folio is a loose composition (though, perhaps, not much looser than *Cymbeline*); and, though there are points of great and truly Shakespearean interest of character in the king and, still more, in Wolsey and queen Katharine, it cannot be said that the character in any one instance, or in all put together, unifies the play as it generally does with Shakespeare. Still, there is no doubt about his authorship in whole or part. No reasonable critic will attempt to go behind the folio as regards plays—though no such critic need accept either 'the whole folio' as regards passages or 'nothing but the folio' in any way. The play is patchy, and some of the patches are inferior; while there are hardly any marks in it of that early and 'first draft' character which we have detected in others.

With the classical plays, we come to a new and very interesting group. In a sense, of course, *Titus Andronicus* belongs to it; but nothing like the extreme earliness of that piece belongs to any of the others, and none of them is mentioned by Meres. Two of them, however, are, internally as well as externally, of very uncertain date; the other three are of Shakespeare's very meridian.

For *Troilus and Cressida*, a licence to print was obtained in 1602/3; but the players objected, and it was not published till half a dozen years later, and then surreptitiously. It is extremely difficult not to believe that it is much older than the earlier date would show. Some of the blank verse, no doubt, is fairly mature: but the author may have furbished this up, and much of it is not mature at all. Instead of transcending his materials, as Shakespeare almost invariably does, he has here failed almost entirely to bring out their possibilities; has not availed himself of Chaucer's beautiful romance so fully as he might; and has dramatised the common Troy-books with a loose yet heavy hand utterly unsuggestive of his maturer craftsmanship. If it were not for certain speeches and touches chiefly in the part of Ulysses, and in the parts of the hero and heroine, it might be called the least Shakespearean of all the plays.

Timon of Athens, again a puzzle, is a puzzle of a different kind. It is usual to resort to the rather Alexandrine suggestion of collaboration and then to put it as late as 1607. To the present writer, the first theory seems unnecessary and the last impossible. There is nothing in *Timon* that Shakespeare, at one time or another, may not have written; there are some things which hardly anybody but Shakespeare can have written; but that he wrote this piece just after *Lear*, even with somebody, not to help, but to hinder, him, is not, from the point of view from which the present survey is written, conceivable. The play is as chaotic as *Troilus*, or more so; and, except Timon himself, it has no character of interest in it. But Timon himself must be Shakespeare's own; he has so much of good in him, and might have been made so much better, that it is impossible to imagine Shakespeare, in his maturity, turning over such a character to be botched by underlings, and associated with third rate company. On the other hand, he might have written the whole play in his nonage and—as in the other case—have thrown in some 'modern touches' to freshen it up and get it off his hands. At any rate, the two plays (which may be called Greek) stand in the sharpest contrast to the great Roman trio, based, in Shakespeare's most easy-going fashion, on North's *Plutarch* for matter, and, sometimes, even for words, but made his own, absolutely and for ever.

None of the three was printed till the folio appeared, though licence appears to have been obtained for *Antony and Cleopatra* in 1608. It is usual to select that date for it and for *Coriolanus*, and to put *Julius Caesar* seven years earlier, because of an apparent allusion to it in that year. Internal evidence does not, perhaps, supply any valid reason for such a separation in date; and, as they are all taken from the same source, they may very well all have been written about the same time. This could not have been very early, from the complete mastery of the blank verse, but might be anywhere after the close of the sixteenth century. All three are masterpieces, but curiously different in kind; though there is an equally curious agreement between them in the manner in which the author, at one time,

71

simply arranges the very words not merely of Plutarch but of North, while, at another, he will add or substitute passages of absolute originality.

Julius Caesar has, at least, this mark of an earlier date that its interest is of a diffused character, and that there is a certain prodigality of poetic passages put in everybody's mouth. The titular hero perishes before half the play is done; and his place is taken, first by Antony and then by Brutus. Nor does he make any very copious appearance even before his murder. Further, the marvellous Shakespearean impartiality seems to take delight in doing the best for each of these heroes in turn; while the prodigality above referred to furnishes not merely the three, Cassius, who is all but a fourth hero, and Portia, but quite insignificant people—Marullus, Casca, Calpurnia—with splendid poetical utterance. The magnificent speech of Antony—all Shakespeare's own; the great exchange of mind between Brutus and Cassius, both as friends and as (almost) foes; the dialogue of Brutus and Portia: these, and many other things, with the surpassing majesty and interest of the theme, have always made the play a great favourite, and deservedly so. Moreover, its central interest from the point of view of romance— the death and revenging of Caesar—is perfect. But, from the point of view of unity of character, which is Shakespeare's general appeal, it may be thought somewhat lacking. Brutus is the only person whose character can supply a continuous tie rod—and, except to those who take the old French Revolution or Roman declamation line of admiration for tyrannicide *per se*, Brutus, admirably as he develops, is rather thin at first. It may plausibly be argued that either he should not have required Cassius's blend of personal and pseudo-patriotic hatred of Caesar to ferment his own patriotism, or he should have detected the insufficiency of the 'lean and hungry' conspirator. Practically, however, *Julius Caesar* is of the panoramic, if not of the kaleidoscopic, order of drama—its appeal is of sequence rather than of composition.

With the other two Roman plays, it is quite different. *Coriolanus* is certainly not deficient in variety of incident, or of personage, but every incident and every personage is, in a way, subservient to the hero. The ordinary descriptions of the *dramatis personae*—'friend to Coriolanus', 'mother to Coriolanus', 'wife to Coriolanus'—acquire a new appositeness from this feature. Menenius and Volumnia are no shadows; the 'gracious silence' herself is all the more gracious for her unobtrusiveness. But it is in relation to Coriolanus that they interest us most. The sordid spite of the tribunes—types well known at this time and at all times—helps to bring out the arrogance, at its worst not sordid, of Caius Martius. The inferior generals set him off. And that interesting, and not very easy, character, Tullus Aufidius, whose psychical evolution Shakespeare has left in obviously intentional uncertainty, furnishes yet another contrast in his real changes from enmity to friendship, and then from hospitality to treachery, with the changes of Coriolanus from the height of Roman patriotism to actual hostility against his ungrateful and degraded country, and from that hostility to semi-reconciliation, at least to the foregoing of his vengeance in obedience to his mother. Most of all do the various mobs—the mob of Rome above all, but, also, the rank and file of the army, the Volscian conspirators, the officers, the senators, the very servants of Aufidius—throw up against their own vulgar variety and characterless commonness the 'headstrong beauty' of the great soldier's mind and will—his hatred of the *vulgus* itself, of its malignity, of its meanness, of its ingratitude. He is, of course, no flawless character: he need not have been rude to the people (one cannot blame him for being so to their misguiders); and, because they committed virtual treason to Rome by banishing its defender, he was certainly not justified in himself committing the overt act. But he remains one of the noblest figures in literature, and his nobility is largely the work of Shakespeare himself. What is more, he has provided Shakespeare with the opportunity of working out a 'one-man' drama, as, except in inferior specimens like *Timon*, he has done nowhere else. For, even in *Hamlet*, the single and peculiar life of the hero does not overshadow all the others, as is done here.

Great as *Coriolanus* is, however, it is not nearly so great as *Antony and Cleopatra*. Coriolanus, personally, is a great figure, but rather narrowly great and hardly as provocative of delight as of admiration.

74

The interest of his story is somewhat lacking in variety, and, cunningly as the comic or serio-comic aspects and interludes are employed to lighten it up, the whole play is rather statuesque. *Antony and Cleopatra* has nearly as infinite a variety as its incomparable heroine herself: its warmth and colour are of the liveliest kind; its character drawing is of the Shakespearean best; the beauties of its versification and diction are almost unparalleled in number, diversity and intensity; and, above all, the powers of the two great poetic motives, love and death, are utilised in it to the utmost possible extent. Even this long list of merits does not exhaust its claims. From the technical side, it is the very type and triumph of the chronicle play—of the kind which dramatises whole years of history, solid portions of the life of man, and keeps them dramatically one by the interwoven threads of character interest, by individual passages of supreme poetry and by scenes or sketches of attaching quality. Here, again, Shakespeare follows North, at times very closely indeed; and here, more than ever, he shows how entirely he is able not to follow his leader when he chooses. The death of Cleopatra, with the ineffable music of the words that follow 'Peace, Peace', is only the strongest example of a pervading fact. But the central interest of character and the side portraits which accompany and enforce it are the greatest points about the play. Nowhere has even Shakespeare given such a pair, hero and heroine, as here. Antony, at once ruined and ennobled by the

75

passion which is both his ἁμαρτία and his abiding
title to sympathy, which completes his friendship for
Caesar in the earlier play; Cleopatra, her frailty
sublimated into the same passion—both heroic in
their very weakness and royal in the way in which
they throw away their royalty: there is nothing like
them anywhere. There is no palliation of fault or of
folly; both are set as plainly before the spectator
as may be, and he will imitate them at his peril. But
the power of romantic tragedy in this direction can
go no further.

It might be questioned whether this power
actually went further in any other direction. But,
possibly, between *Julius Caesar* and the other two
Roman plays—certainly in the same general period,
and, according to popular reckoning, between 1602
and 1605—Shakespeare produced, it is thought in
the order to be named, what are pre-eminently the
four wheels of his chariot, the four wings of his
spirit, in the tragic and tragicomic division, *Hamlet,
Othello, Macbeth* and *Lear*. To condense the enormous
mass of discussion on these, and especially on the
first, were here impossible. The puzzles of the text
of *Hamlet* (which differs most remarkably in the
quarto of 1603, apparently pirated, in that of 1604,
which at least claims authenticity, and in that of the
folio), though perhaps less than they seem, and
much less than they have been thought to be, are
considerable; and the problems of the play are
infinite. Its immediate, lasting and now world-wide
popularity is not surprising. For, though Hamlet

himself is capable of being problematised to the nth, he is a sufficiently taking figure (especially as introduced by the ghost scenes) to persons who care little indeed for problems. The enormous length of the play is diversified by the most varied, and, at times, most exciting, action. In the common phrase, there is something for everyone—the supernatural, the death of Polonius, that of Ophelia, the fight or almost fight in the churchyard, the duel, the final slaughter scene (simply an exciting moment for the mere vulgar)—the pity of all these things for the sentimental, the poetry of them for those who can appreciate it. And, above all, and with all, there is the supreme interest of the character presentment, which informs and transforms the incidents, and which, not merely in the central figure, is the richest and most full to be found in Shakespeare. This may be developed in one instance.

It has been impossible, in the scale and range of the present notice, to dwell on individual characters. But, putting sheer poetical expression aside, the Shakespearean character is the Shakespearean note; and, for more reasons than one, it would be an incorrectness not to offer a specimen of dealing with this feature. No better suggests itself than the character of Claudius. For it seems to have escaped even some elect wits; and it is very typical. There were at least two ways in which an ordinary, or rather more than ordinary, dramatist might have dealt with this other 'majesty of Denmark'. He could have been made a crude dramatic villain—a

77

crowned 'Shakebag' or 'Black Will', to use the phraseology of his creator's own day. He could have been made pure straw—a mere common usurper. And it would appear that he has actually seemed to some to be one or other of these two. Neither of them is the Claudius which Shakespeare has presented; and those who take him as either seem to miss the note which, putting sheer poetic faculty once more aside, is the note of Shakespeare. It is not to be supposed that Shakespeare liked Claudius; if he did, and if he has produced on respectable readers the effect above hinted at, he certainly was as ineffectual a writer as the merest *crétin*, or the merest crank, among his critics could imagine. But neither did he dislike Claudius; he knew that, in the great Greek phrase, it was the duty of creators to 'see fair'—τὰ ἴσα νέμειν—in the handling of their creations. It would appear that the successor of Hamlet I might have been a very respectable person, if his brother had not possessed a kingdom and a queen that he wanted for himself. But this brother did, unluckily, possess these things and the Claudian—not ἁμαρτία, not 'tragic frailty', but outrageous, unforgivable, fully punished— crime was that he would not tolerate this possession. He put an end to it, and—let those laugh at him who like—he seems to have thought that he could trammel up the consequence. Macbeth was wiser. If it were not for the ugly circumstances and the illegitimate assistance of the ghost, we might be rather sorry for Claudius at first. There was nothing out of the way in the succession of brother before son. There was nothing (except, perhaps, undue haste) out of the way, under the dispensation of dispensations, in the successive marriage of one woman to two brothers. Fifty years before Shakespeare's birth, queen Katharine did it, and few people thought or think her other than a saint. A hundred years after Shakespeare's birth, Louise de Gonzague, queen of Poland, did it, and nobody thought the worse of her at all. It is clear that there was not much likelihood of offspring from the second marriage: even Hamlet himself, in the very scene where his abusive description of the king ('not evidence', if ever anything was not) has prejudiced many against Claudius, seems to admit this. Claudius himself would probably—his very words could be cited—have been most happy to regard Hamlet as crown prince, would not have objected to receive Ophelia (perhaps with a slight protest against derogation) as crown princess and, after a due enjoyment of his kingdom and his wife, to assign the former to them and die quite comfortably.

But this could not be: the gods would not have 'seen fair' if they had allowed it, and the πρώταρχος ἄτη of the crime in the orchard bears its fruit. Yet Claudius behaves himself by no means ill. He meets Hamlet's early, and, as yet, ungrounded, or only half grounded, sulks with a mixture of dignity and kindness which is admirable in a difficult situation. There does not appear any prejudice against Hamlet (though, of course, guilt makes the king uneasy)

79

when Polonius first tells him of the prince's antics. When he has eavesdropped, a proceeding fully justified by the statecraft of the time, his desire to get rid of Hamlet, somehow, is natural, and it does not yet appear that he has any design to 'get rid' of him in criminal kind. Even after the play—an outrageous insult in any case—there is no sign of murderous purpose either in his words to Rosencrantz and Guildenstern or in the prayer soliloquy. Only after the killing of Polonius, which might have alarmed an innocent man, does he decide on the *literae Bellerophontis*. Few who have paid any attention to it have denied the combined courage and skill with which he meets the *émeute* headed by Laertes. Even thenceforward, he is not pure villain, and, though it endangers all his plans, he tries to save the queen, between whom and himself it is quite certain that a real affection exists. He is a villain, but he is a man; and there are probably lesser villains who are rather poorer personages as men. Now, is this mere whitewashing on the critic's part, or the puerile and sneaking kindness for villany which is not quite unknown in men of letters? Not at all. No better deserved swordthrust was ever given than Hamlet's last; and Shakespeare never palliates the crime of Claudius in the very least degree. But he knows that a criminal is not necessarily bad all through; and he knows that there is no cheaper or falser morality than that which thinks that you must represent a criminal as bad all through lest you tempt people to sympathise with his crime. May it be added that, at this time of his career, he simply could not 'scamp' his work in the direction of character any more than in the direction of poetry? Others might throw in 'supers' to fill up a play—he would not. Claudius, of course, in no way disputes the position of hero; but there is stuff in him, as he is presented, for half a dozen heroes of the Racinian type.

Of Ophelia, and Polonius, and the queen and all the rest, not to mention Hamlet himself (in whose soul it would be absurd to attempt to discover new points here), after this we need not say anything. But it is observable that they are not, as in the case of Coriolanus, interesting merely or mainly for their connection with the hero, but in themselves. And it must be added that, not merely in the soliloquies and set speeches, but in the dialogue, even in its least important patchwork, Shakespeare's mastery of blank verse has reached complete perfection.

If *Othello* came next, as it may very well have done—it has been asserted, on the faith of a document not now producible, to have been acted at court on 1 November 1604—there was certainly no falling off. The pity, if not the terror, is made more intense than even in *Hamlet*. And, though for complexity Iago cannot approach Hamlet, he is almost as interesting. Once more, the Shakespearean impartiality is shown in this character. Iago, in the ordinary sense, is a much 'worse' man than Claudius; and, unlike Claudius, he has no compunction. But you see his point of view. It is by no means so certain as some critics have thought that his suspicions of Othello and Emilia are merely pretended; it is quite certain that he has never forgiven, and never will forgive, Othello or Cassio for the preference accorded by the former to the latter. Against Desdemona, he probably has no personal spite whatsoever; but she is the most convenient instrument that suggests itself for embroiling his two foes with each other and plaguing them both; so he uses her, once more without compunction of any kind. Roderigo is another instrument and a useful pigeon as well. But this newer 'ancient'—very different from Pistol!—has an admirable intellect, a will of steel and a perfectly dauntless courage. 'I bleed, sir; but not killed' is one of the greatest speeches in Shakespeare, and the innocent commentators who have asked whether Shakespeare 'did not hate Iago' can never have apprehended it. As for Desdemona herself, an interesting point arises in connection with another of Shakespeare's most pity-claiming figures, Cordelia, and may be noticed when we come to her.

Those who (if there be any such) believe that Shakespeare wrote the whole of *Macbeth* and that he wrote it about 1605, must have curious standards of criticism. To believe that he wrote the whole of it is quite easy—indeed, the present writer has little or no doubt on the matter; but the belief is only possible on the supposition that it was written at rather different times. The second scene, that in which the 'bleeding sergeant' appears, and some few other passages, are, in verse and phrase, whole stages older than the bulk of the play, which, in these respects, is fully equal to its great companions. The character interest is limited to the hero and heroine. But in the thane and king—who is a marvellous variant sketch of Hamlet, except that *he* can never leave off, while Hamlet can never begin, and that, also, he can never leave off metaphysicalising on the things he does, while Hamlet's similar self-indulgence is confined to those he does not do— its intensity and variety yield only to that of Hamlet himself; while Lady Macbeth is quite peerless. And the fresh handling of the supernatural illustrates, fortunately not for the last time, the curious fertility of the writer in a direction where, especially when it is blended with events and motives not supernatural, failure is not so much the usual, as the invariable, result. That the Shakespeare of one play, or part, should be the Shakespeare of another, is a constantly repeated marvel; but it is scarcely anywhere more marvellous than in the fact that the same writer wrote *A Midsummer Night's Dream, Hamlet, Macbeth* and *The Tempest*.

Early British history seems at this moment to have had a fascination for Shakespeare; for *Macbeth* appears to have been followed pretty quickly by *King Lear*, and the date of *Cymbeline* cannot have been very distant as it was certainly a stage play in 1610. *King Lear*, like its companions in the great *quatuor*, has special virtues, but it resembles them and *Antony and Cleopatra* in a certain regality of tone which

83

hardly appears elsewhere. It resembles *Othello*, also, in being a tragedy of pity above all things; and it offers, perhaps, the most notable opportunity for the examination of the Shakespearean ἁμαρτία, which at once agrees and contrasts strikingly with the Aristotelian. The terrible fate of Lear—which the poet wisely introduced instead of the happy (or differently unhappy) ending which occurs in the chronicles and in a worthless contemporary play, a little earlier than his own—may seem excessive. As a punishment for his selfish abandonment and par-celling out of the kingdom, his general petulance and his blind misjudgment of his daughters, it may be so; as the consequence of his frailty, not. So, too, Cordelia's disinheritance and her ultimate fate are caused (whether deserved or not is, as before, a different question) by her self-willed and excessive want of compliance with her father's foolish, but not wholly unnatural, craving for professions of affec-tion. The calamities of Gloster are a little more in the way of strict poetical justice of the ordinary kind; but they coincide well enough. The character of Edmund is a pendant to that of Iago, and his final speeches 'The wheel is come full circle: I am here', and 'Yet Edmund was beloved', are even more revealing than the stoical finale of the ancient. The extraordinary success of the fool has never been denied save by his unofficial successors; nor the superhuman poetry of the heath scenes. That the tragedy is too tragical, may be an argument against tragedy, or against the theatre generally; but not against this play. The one accusation of some weight is the horror of the Gloster mutilation scene, a survival of the old *Andronicus* days which, in a way, is interesting, but which, perhaps, could have been spared. The fact that it actually is a survival is the most interesting thing about it, except the other fact that it shocks, as, in an earlier play, it certainly would not. Nothing can show better the enormous lift which Shakespeare had himself given to the stage in, at most, some fifteen years, than the demand made on him, by modern criticism, not to do what everyone had been doing.

Last come the famous three: *Cymbeline, The Winter's Tale* and *The Tempest*, where no idle fancy has seen 'the calmed and calming *mens adepta*' of which one of all but the greatest of Shakespeare's contemporaries, Fulke Greville, speaks in a great passage of prose. The first and second were seen by Simon Forman, an astrologer of the day, in 1610 and 1611; *The Tempest* was certainly performed in 1613, and may have been written one or two years earlier—a theory which makes it not a late play at all is absurd and rebutted by the whole internal evidence. But internal coincides with external in allotting the three to the latest period possible: the versification supporting the general tone, and the intense romantic influence corroborating both. In respect of construction, however, there is a remarkable difference between *Cymbeline* and *The Winter's Tale*, on the one hand, and *The Tempest*, on the other.

Cymbeline has by some been reproached with being,

and by others regretfully admitted to be, the loosest and most disorderly play in Shakespeare. Not only does he take his largest romantic licence of neglecting unity of time and place—to that the reader must long have been accustomed. Not only does he mix plots and interests with the most *insouciant* liberality, as if he were making a salad of them. But he leaves his materials, his personages, his incidents, at a perfect tangle of loose ends. Still, the interest is maintained, partly because of the actual attraction of many of his episodes; partly because of the exquisite poetry which is showered upon the play in every direction; but, most of all, because of the perfect charm of the character of the heroine. That Shakespeare has equalled Imogen is certainly true; but he has never surpassed her, and he has never repeated or anticipated her.

Perhaps there is nothing more remarkable in these three plays, even among Shakespeare's work, than the extraordinary beauty—both in phrase, passage and scene—of their separate parts. The word 'beauty' is used advisedly. Here, in *Cymbeline*, for instance, fault may be found—irrelevantly, perhaps, but not ungroundedly—with construction, with connection of scenes and so forth. But those who look, not at the skeleton, but at the body, not at the mathematical proportion of features, but at the countenance, will hardly be disturbed by this. The two Imogen and Iachimo scenes; the whole episode of Belarius and his supposed sons; the miraculous song dirge which Collins, though he made a pretty thing of it, merely

86

prettified—these are things impossible to conceive as bettered, difficult to imagine as equalled, or approached.

The Winter's Tale has something, but less, of the same sublime neglect of meticulous accuracy of construction; it has, perhaps, a more varied interest; it has even more lavishness of poetical appeal. The 'sea coast of Bohemia' is nothing; but the story, merely as a story, is certainly more romantic than dramatic. There is no character that approaches Imogen; for Perdita, exquisite as she is, has no character, properly speaking. The jealousy of Leontes, though an interesting variant on that of Othello, and that of Posthumus, not to say on that of Master Ford, has a certain touch of ferocious stupidity, which Shakespeare probably intended, but which is not engaging. Hermione, admirable so far as she goes, is not quite fully shown to us; and, though Paulina is a capital portrait of what Ben Jonson declared his own wife to be—'a shrew but honest'—she does not go far. Autolycus, perhaps, is the only figure who fully displays the Shakespearean completeness. But the fascination of the play is quite independent of these knots in the reed. The abundance of it—the cheerful beginning and sombre close of the first Sicilian scenes; the partly tragic opening and pastoral continuation of the Bohemian; the tragicomedy and *coup de théâtre* of the end—is very great. But the suffusion of the whole with quintessenced poetry in the fashion just mentioned is greater. It appears chiefly in flash of phrase for

87

the first three acts till the great storm scene at the end of the third, with the rather severe punishment of Antigonus and the contrasted farce of the shepherds. But, in the fourth, where comedy and romance take the place of farce and tragedy, and especially in Perdita's famous flower speech, it overflows; and there is plenty of it in the fifth. Had Greene lived to see this dramatising of his story, he might have been more angry than ever with the upstart crow; if, as sometimes, though too seldom, happens, his stormy spring had settled into a mellow early autumn, he ought to have been reconciled.

But, while the charms of *Cymbeline* and *The Winter's Tale* appear in even greater measure in *The Tempest*, this astonishing swan song is open to none of the objections which, from some points of view, may lie against them. It is almost regular, so far as 'time' is concerned; its violation of 'place' is very small, being confined to the limits of one little island; and its 'action' though, of course, of the English multiple kind, can be plausibly argued to be almost single in its multiplicity. The working of the spells of Prospero on all the important members of the shipwrecked crew in their diverse natures, qualities and importance—for correction on Alonso, Antonio and Sebastian (though these last two were probably incorrigible); for trial and reward on Ferdinand; for well deserved plaguing on Stephano and Trinculo—might have given more pause to Aristotle 'if he had seen ours', as Dryden says, than anything else. The contrast of Caliban and Ariel is almost classical in conception, though ultraromantic in working out. The loves of Ferdinand and Miranda at once repair and confirm according to justice the acquisition of Milan by Naples, which has been unjustly accomplished before the opening. In the management of the supernatural, too, Shakespeare once more shows that unique combination of power and economy which has been noted. But he has not, because of this extra expenditure—if, indeed, it was an extra expenditure—of trouble, in the very least stinted the outpouring of beauty on individual character, scene, passage, phrase or line. Ariel and Caliban among super- or extra-natural personages, and Miranda, even among Shakespeare's women, occupy positions of admitted supremacy. Prospero is of extraordinary subtlety; the butler and the jester are among the best of their excellent class. It is curious that this play makes a kind of pendant to *Much Ado About Nothing* in the nearness with which comedy approaches tragedy, though the supernatural element relieves the spectator of the apprehension which, in the other case, is not unjustified. The inset masque, too (to which there is a faint parallel in *Cymbeline*), is a remarkable feature, and adds to the complicated, and yet not disorderly, attractions of the piece. But these attractions are all-pervading. The versification, though in part of Shakespeare's latest style, is of his best, in song and dialogue alike, throughout; and there are curious side interests in Gonzalo's citation of Montaigne, and in other matters. But the main charm is once more in the poetry, to which the prose adds not a little. The vividness of the storm; the admirable *protasis* of Miranda and Prospero; Ariel, whenever he speaks, and Caliban not seldom —give this charm, while Prospero himself is always a master of it. Indeed, in the great parallel with Calderon of 'life's a dream', led up to by the picture of the vanishing universe, it reaches one of the 'topless towers' of poetry. To refuse to see an actual leavetaking in this perfect creation with its (to say the least) remarkable prophecy of the 'burial of the book' is, surely, an idle scepticism, considering the weight of positive evidence of all kinds which supports the idea. At any rate, if it were not the last, it ought to have been; and, though there are too many instances of non-coincidence between what ought to be and what is, we need hardly lay it down as a rule that what ought to have been could not be. *The Tempest* is not all Shakespeare: only all Shakespeare is that. But it may, at least, be pronounced a diploma piece of Shakespeare's art.

The foregoing survey of Shakespeare's plays has been made rather from the results of a long and intimate familiarity with their contents, than in reference to traditional opinion in their favour, or to recent efforts in the opposite direction. Some of these latter, such as the attacks of the very remarkable young Breton critic Ernest Hello not long since, and those of Tolstoy, only the other day, have been made, seriously and in good faith, from points of view which, when allowed for, deprive them of most of their effect. Others have come from mere mountebankery, or from the more respectable, but not much more valuable, desire to be unlike other people. But, apparently, they have had the effect of inducing some critics who are nearer to the truth to make provisos and qualifications—to return, in fact, to something like the attitude of George III, that 'a great deal of Shakespeare is sad stuff, only one must not say so', but to put on more show of courage than the king and dare to 'say so', with more or less excuse for theatrical necessities, 'faults of the time', journeyman's work executed as a mere matter of business and the like. Perhaps this is only a new form of cant. For the characteristics of the time something, of course, must be allowed; with, however, the remembrance that, after all, they may not be faults when brought *sub specie aeternitatis*. But, except in the very earliest plays—not half a dozen out of the whole seven and thirty—and in passages of the middle division, it may almost be said that there is *no* 'sad stuff' in Shakespeare, though there is a great deal of very sad stuff in what has been written about him. In particular, both the impugners and the defenders on the theatrical side seem to protest too much. It is, of course, quite true that all Shakespeare's plays were written to be acted; but it may be questioned whether this is much more than an accident, arising from the fact that the drama was the dominant form of literature. It was a happy accident, because of the unique opportunity which this form gives of employing both the vehicles of poetry and of prose. But, though in a far milder degree, it was unlucky, because nothing has varied more or more quickly than the popular taste in drama, and, therefore, dramatic work has been exposed to even greater vicissitudes than those which necessarily await all literary performance. Even here, its exceptional excellence is evidenced curiously enough by the fact that there has been no time—the last forty years of the seventeenth century are not a real exception—at which Shakespeare has not (sometimes, it is true, in more or less travestied forms) retained popularity even on the stage.

But, if we regard his work from the far more permanent, and less precarious, standpoint of literary criticism, his exceptional greatness can be shown in divers and striking ways. The chain of literary dictators who have borne witness to it in their several fashions and degrees—Ben Jonson, Dryden, Pope, Samuel Johnson, Coleridge—has been pointed out often enough. It has not, perhaps, been pointed out quite so often that the reservations of these great critics, when they make them, and the more or less unqualified disapproval of others, can always be traced to some practically disabling cause. Ben Jonson held a different theory of the drama; Dryden, for a time, at least, was led aside by the heroic play and, for another time, by the delusion that the manners, language and so forth of 'the present day' must be an improvement on those of yesterday; Pope, by something not dissimilar to that which worked in Dryden's case, and Johnson, by something not dissimilar to that which worked in Jonson's; Coleridge, by 'his fun'—that is to say, by occasional crotchet and theory. On the other hand, Voltaire, with all who followed him, differed partly in point of view, and partly was influenced by the half concealed, half open conviction that French literature must be supreme. Patriotism worked in another way on Rümelin, vexed at the way in which his countrymen, led by the Schlegels (from the earlier, and too much forgotten, John Elias onwards) and Goethe, had deified foreigners. Hello was affected by that strange dread and distrust of great human art which has influenced the Roman Catholic church almost as much as the extreme protestant sects, and which descends from Plato through the Fathers. The mere dissident for the sake of dissent need hardly be noticed; still less the mountebanks. But it is a certificate of genuineness to have mountebanks against you; and the heretic, by the fact of his heresy, goes further than he knows to establish the orthodoxness of orthodoxy.

Except from the historical side, however, it is unnecessary to dwell on this part of the matter. What establishes the greatness of Shakespeare is the substance of Shakespeare's work. 'Take and read' is the very best advice that can be given in reference to him. It is not necessary, nor at all desirable, to disparage at least part of the enormous labour that has been spent upon him by others. But it is quite certain that anyone who, with fair education and competent wits, gives his days and nights to the reading of the actual plays will be a far better judge than anyone who allows himself to be distracted by comment and controversy. The important thing is to get the Shakespearean atmosphere, to feel the breath of the Shakespearean spirit. And it is doubtful whether it is not much safer to get this first, and at first hand, than to run the risk of not getting it while investigating the exact meaning of every allusion and the possible date of every item. The more thoroughly and impartially this spirit is observed and extracted, the more will it be found to consist in the subjection of all things to what may be called the romantic process of presenting them in an atmosphere of poetical suggestion rather than as sharply defined and logically stated. But this romantic process is itself characterised and pervaded by a philosophical depth and width of conception of life which is not usually associated with romance. And it is enlivened and made actual by the dramatic form which, whether by separable or inseparable accident, the writer has adopted. Thus, Shakespeare —as no one had done before him, and as people have done since far more often in imitation of him than independently—unites the powers and advantages of three great forms: the romance (in verse or prose), pure poetry and the drama. The first gives him variety, elasticity, freedom from constraint and limit. The second enables him to transport. The third at once preserves his presentations from the excessive vagueness and vastness which non-dramatic ro-

94

mance invites, and helps him to communicate actuality and vividness.

It is in the examination of his treatment, now of individual incidents and personages, now of complicated stories, by the aid of these combined in-. struments, that the most profitable, as well as the most delightful, study of Shakespeare consists. But there is no doubt that, as a result of this study, two things emerge as his special gifts. The first is the coinage of separate poetic phrases; the second is the construction and getting into operation of individual and combined character. In a third point—the telling of a story or the construction of a drama—he is far greater than is often allowed. After his earliest period, there is very little in any play that does not directly bear upon the main plot in his sense of that word. Even in so very long, so very complicated, a piece as *Hamlet*, it is almost impossible to 'cut' without loss—to the intelligent and unhasting reader, at any rate, if not to the eager or restless spectator. But plot, in his sense, means, mainly—not entirely— the evolution of character; and so we may return to that point.

Two features strike us in Shakespearean character drawing which are not so prominent in any other. The one is its astonishing prodigality, the other its equally astonishing thoroughness, regard being had to the purpose of the presentation. On this latter head, reference may be made to the examination of the character of Claudius above given; but it would be perfectly easy to supplement this by scores, nay,

95

literally, by hundreds, of others, were there space for it. Shakespeare never throws away a character; but, at the same time, he never scamps one that is in any way necessary or helpful to his scheme. But this thoroughness, of course, shows itself more fully still in his great personages. It has been almost a stumblingblock—the bounty of the describing detail being so great that interpreters have positively lost themselves in it. Nor was this probably unintended; for Shakespeare knew human nature too well to present the narrow unmistakable type character which belongs to a different school of drama. His methods of drawing character are numerous. The most obvious of them is the soliloquy. This has been found fault with as unnatural—but only by those who do not know nature. The fact is that the soliloquy is so universal that it escapes observers who are not acute and active. Everybody, except persons of quite abnormal hebetude, 'talks to himself as he walks by himself, and thus to himself says he'. According to temperament and intellect, he is more or less frank with himself; but his very attempts to deceive himself are more indicative of character than his bare actions. The ingenious idea of the 'palace of truth' owes all its ingenuity and force to this fact. Now, Shakespeare has constituted his work, in its soliloquies, as a vast palace of truth, in which those characters who are important enough are compelled thus to reveal themselves. Nothing contributes quite so much to the solidity and completeness of his system of developing plot by the development of character; nor does anything display more fully the extraordinary power and range, the 'largeness and universality', of his own soul. For the soliloquy, like all weapons or instruments which unite sharpness and weight, is an exceedingly difficult and dangerous one to wield. It may very easily be overdone in the novel (where there are not the positive checks on it which the drama provides) even more than in the drama itself. It is very difficult to do well. And there is a further danger even for those who can do it well and restrain themselves from overdoing it: that the soliloquies will represent not the character but the author; that they will assist in building up for us, if we desire it, the nature of Brown or Jones, but will not do very much for the construction or revelation of that of Brown's or Jones's heroes and heroines. Shakespeare has avoided or overcome all these points. His soliloquies, or set speeches of a soliloquial character, are never, in the mature plays, overdone; they are never futile or unnatural; and, above all, they are so variously adapted to the idiosyncrasies of the speakers that, while many people have tried to distil an essence of Shakespeare out of them, nobody has succeeded. From Thackeray's famous *parabases* (even when they are put in the mouths of his characters as they sometimes are) we learn very little more about these characters than he has told us or will tell us in another way; but we learn to know himself almost infallibly. From Shakespeare's soliloquies we hardly see him even in a glass darkly; but we see the characters who are made to utter them as plain as the handwriting upon the wall.

It remains to consider three points of great, though varying, importance—Shakespeare's morality in the wide sense, his versification and his style.

In dealing with the first, there is no necessity to dwell much on the presence in his work of 'broad' language and 'loose' scenes. That he exceeds in this way far less than most of his contemporaries will only be denied by those who do not really know the Elizabethan drama. Of the excess itself, it seems rather idle to say much. The horror which it excites in some cases is, perhaps, as much a matter of fashion as the original delinquency. But this is only a miserable specialisation and belittlement of the word 'morality'. In the larger sense, Shakespeare's morals are distinguished and conditioned almost equally by sanity, by justice and by tolerance. He is not in the least squeamish—as has been said, he shocks many as not being squeamish enough—but he never, except in *All's Well that Ends Well*, and, perhaps, *Measure for Measure*, has an unhealthy plot or even an unhealthy situation. His justice is of the so-called 'poetical' kind, but not in the least of the variety often so misnamed. In fact, as a rule, he is rather severe—in some cases, decidedly so—and, though too much of an artist to court the easy tragedy of the unhappy ending, is, except in his last three plays, equally proof against the seductions of the happy sort. But this severity is tempered by, and throws into relief, the third quality of tolerance in which he excels every other author. This tolerance is not complaisance: justice prevents that, and sanity too. Shakespeare never winks at anything. But, as he understands everything, so, without exactly pardoning it ('that's when he's tried above'), he invariably adopts a strictly impartial attitude towards everything and everybody. In this, he stands in marked contrast to Dante, who, with almost equal sanity and fully equal justice, is not merely unnecessarily inexorable, but distinctly partisan—not merely a hanging judge, but a hanging judge doubled with an unsparing public prosecutor. It was once observed as an *obiter dictum* by a Dante scholar of unsurpassed competence[1] that 'Dante *knows* he is unfair'. It might be said that the extraordinary serenity and clarity of Shakespeare's mind and temper make it unnecessary for him to think whether he is fair or not. He gives the character as it is—the other characters and the reader may make what they can of it. He allows Malcolm to call Macbeth a 'dead butcher' and Lady Macbeth a 'fiendlike queen', because it is what Malcolm would have done. But he does not attach these tickets to them; and you will accept the said tickets at your own risk. Another contrast which is useful is, again, that of Thackeray. The author of *Vanity Fair* and *The Newcomes* has a power of vivifying

[1] [A. J. Butler.]

character not much inferior to Shakespeare's. But, when he has vivified his characters, he descends too much into the same arena with them; and he likes or dislikes them, as one likes or dislikes fellow creatures, not as the creator should be affected towards creations. Becky Sharp is a very fallible human creature, and Barnes Newcome is a detestable person. But Thackeray is hard on Becky; and, though he tries not to be hard on Barnes, he is. Shakespeare is never hard on any of his characters—not merely in the cases of Lady Macbeth and Cleopatra, where there is no difficulty; but in those of Iago and Edmund, of Richard and of John, where there is. The difficulty does not exist for him. And yet he has no sneaking kindness for the bad, great person as Milton has. The potter has made the pot as the pot ought to be and could not but be; he does not think it necessary to label it 'caution' or 'this is a bad pot', much less to kick it into potsherds. If it breaks itself, it must; in the sherds into which it breaks itself, in those it will lie; and 'there is namore to seyn'.

Equally matter subject to opinion, but matter much more difficult to pronounce upon with even tolerable distinctness and trenchancy, is the feature of style. It is, perhaps, in this point that Shakespeare is most distinguished from the other greatest writers. He has mannerisms; but they are mostly worn as clothes—adopted or discarded for fashion's or season's sake. He has no mannerism in the sense of natural or naturalised gesture which is recognisable at once. When we say that a phrase is Shake-spearean, it is rather because of some supreme and curiously simple felicity than because of any special 'hall-mark', such as exists in Milton and even in Dante. Even Homer has more mannerism than Shakespeare, whose greatest utterances—Prospero's epilogue to the masque, Cleopatra's death words, the crispest sayings of Beatrice and Touchstone, the passion of Lear, the reveries of Hamlet, others too many even to catalogue—bear no relation to each other in mere expression, except that each is the most appropriate expression for the thought. Eu-phuism and word play, of course, are very frequent—shockingly frequent, to some people, it would seem. But they are merely things that the poet plays at—whether for his own amusement or his readers', or both, is a question, perhaps of some curiosity, but of no real importance. The well-ascertained and extra-ordinary copiousness of his vocabulary is closely connected with this peculiar absence of peculiarity in his style. The writer given to mannerism neces-sarily repeats, if not particular words, particular forms of phrases—notoriously, in some cases, parti-cular words also. The man who, in all cases, is to suit his phrase to his meaning, not his meaning to his phrase, cannot do this. Further, Shakespeare, like almost all good English writers, though to the persistent displeasure of some good English critics, coins words with the utmost freedom, merely observing sound analogy. He shows no preference for 'English' over 'Latin' vocabulary, nor any the other way. But, no doubt, he appreciates, and he certainly employs, the advantages offered by their contrast, as in the capital instance of

> The multitudinous seas incarnadine
> Making the green one red,

where all but the whole of the first line is Aristotle's *xenon* and the whole of the next clause his *kyrion*. In fact, it is possible to talk about Shakespeare's style for ever, but impossible in any way to define it. It is practically 'allstyle', as a certain condiment is called 'allspice'; and its universality justifies the Buffonian definition—even better, perhaps, that earlier one of Shakespeare's obscure Spanish contemporary Alfonso Garcia Matamoros as *habitus orationis a cujusque natura fluens*.

There is no need to acknowledge defeat, in this way, as regards the last point to be handled, Shakespeare's versification. This, while it is of the highest importance for the arrangement of his work, requires merely a little attention to the prosody of his predecessors, and a moderate degree of patient and intelligent observation, to make it comparatively plain sailing. In no respect is the Meres list of more importance than in this; for, though it does not arrange its own items in order, it sets them definitely against the others as later, and enables us, by observing the differences between the groups as wholes, to construct the order of sequence between individual plays. Hardly less valuable is the practical certainty that *The Winter's Tale, Cymbeline* and *The Tempest* are the latest plays, and, to say the least, the extreme probability of the grouping of the greatest of the others as belonging to a short period immediately before and a rather longer period immediately after the meeting of the centuries.

Putting these facts together with the certain conditions of prosody in the plays of the Marlowe group, and in the nondescripts of the third quarter of the sixteenth century, we are in a condition to judge Shakespeare's progress in versification with fair safety. For the earliest period, we have pieces like *Love's Labour's Lost* and *The Comedy of Errors* on the one hand, like *Titus Andronicus* on the other. In this last, we see an attempt to play the game of the Marlowe heroic, the unrimed 'drumming decasyllabon', strictly and uncompromisingly. The verses are turned out like bullets, singly from the mould; there is little condescendence (though there is some) to rime, even at the end of scenes and tirades; there is no prose proper. But there is considerable variation of pause; and, though the inflexibility of the line sound is little affected by it, there is a certain running over of sense in which, especially when conjoined with the pause, there is promise for the future.

The two other plays represent a quite different order of experiment. *Love's Labour's Lost*, especially, is a perfect *macédoine* of metres. There is blank verse, and plenty of it, and sometimes very good, though always inclining to the 'single-mould'. But there is also abundance of rime; plenty of prose; arrangement in stanza, especially quatrain; doggerel, some-

103

times refining itself to tolerably regular anapaests; fourteeners; octosyllables or, rather, the octosyllable shortened catalectically and made trochaic; finally, pure lyric of the most melodious kind. The poet has not made up his mind which is the best instrument and is trying all—not, in every case, with a certain touch, but, in every case, with a touch which brings out the capacities of the instrument itself as it has rarely, if ever, been brought out before.

In the other early plays, with a slight variation in proportion to subject, and with regard to the fact whether they are adaptations or not, this process of promiscuous experiment and, perhaps, half unconscious selection continues. The blank verse steadily improves and, by degrees, shakes off any suggestion of the chain, still more of the tale of bullets, and acquires the astonishing continuity and variety of its best Shakespearean form. Still, it constantly relapses into rime—often for long passages and, still oftener, at the ends or breaks of scenes and at the conclusion of long speeches; sometimes, perhaps, merely to give a cue; sometimes, to emphasise a sentiment or call attention to an incident or an appearance. The very stanza is not relinquished; it appears in *Romeo and Juliet*, in *A Midsummer Night's Dream*, even in *The Merchant of Venice*. The doggerel and the fourteeners, except when the latter are used (as they sometimes are) to extend and diversify the blank verse itself, gradually disappear; but the octosyllabic, and more directly lyrical, insets are used freely. The point, however, in that which is, probably, the latest of this batch, and in the whole of the great central group of comedies and tragedies, is the final selection of blank verse itself for reliance, and its development. Not only, as has just been noticed, do the deficiencies of the form in its earlier examples— its stiffness, its want of fluency and symphony, the gasps, as it has been put, of a pavior with the lifting and setting down of his rammer—not only do these defects disappear, but the merits and capabilities of the form appear contrariwise in ways for which there is no precedent in prosodic history. The most important of these, for the special dramatic purpose, if also the most obvious, is the easy and unforced breaking up of the line itself for the purpose of dialogue. But this, of course, had been done with many metres before; even medieval octosyllable writers had had no difficulty with it, though the unsuitableness of rime for dialogue necessarily appeared. But Shakespeare enlarged greatly and boldly on their practice. In all his mature plays— *Hamlet* is a very good example to use for illustration —the decasyllabic or five-foot norm is rather a norm than a positive rule. He always, or almost always, makes his lines, whether single, continuous, or broken, referable to this norm. But he will cut them down to shorter, or extend them to greater, length without the least hesitation. Alexandrines are frequent and fourteeners not uncommon, on the one hand; octosyllables and other fractions equally usual. But all adjust themselves to the five-foot scheme; and the pure examples of that scheme preponderate so that there is no danger of its being confused or mistaken.

Secondly, the lines, by manipulation of pause and of *enjambement* or overrunning, are induced to compose a continuous symphonic run—not a series of gasps. In some passages—for instance, the opening lines of *Antony and Cleopatra*—the pause will hardly be found identical in any two of a considerable batch of verses. As to its location, the poet entirely disregards the centripetal rule dear to critics at almost all times. He sometimes disregards it to the extent—horrible to the straiter sect of such critics—of putting a heavy pause at the first or at the ninth syllable. Always, in his middle period, he practises what he taught to Milton—the secret of the verse period and paragraph—though in drama he has a greater liberty still of beginning this and ending it at any of his varied pause places, without troubling himself whether these places begin and end a line or not. Sometimes, indeed, he seems to prefer that they should not coincide.

But the third peculiarity which distinguishes the accomplished blank verse of Shakespeare is the most important of all. It is the mastery—on good principles of English prosody from the thirteenth century onwards, but in the teeth of critical dicta in his own day and for centuries to follow—of trisyllabic substitution. By dint of this, the cadence of the line is varied, and its capacity is enlarged, in the former case to an almost infinite, in the latter to a very great, extent. Once more, the decasyllabic norm is kept—is, in fact, religiously observed. But the play of the verse, the spring and reach and flexibility of it, are as that of a good fishing-rod to that of a brass curtain-pole. The measure is never really loose—it never in the least approaches doggerel. But it has absolute freedom: no sense that it wishes to convey, and no sound that it wishes to give as accompaniment to that sense, meet the slightest check or jar in their expression.

In the latest division, one of the means of variation which had been used even before Shakespeare, and freely by him earlier, assumes a position of paramount and, perhaps, excessive importance, which it maintains in successors and pupils like Fletcher, and which, perhaps, carries with it dangerous possibilities. This is what is sometimes called the feminine, or, in still more dubious phrase, the 'weak', ending; but what may be better, and much more expressively, termed the redundant syllable. That, with careful, and rather sparing, use it adds greatly to the beauty of the measure, there is no doubt at all: the famous Florizel and Perdita scene in *The Winter's Tale* is but one of many instances. But it is so convenient and so easy that it is sure to be abused; and abused it was, not, perhaps, by Shakespeare, but certainly by Fletcher. And something worse than mere abuse, destruction of the measure itself, and the substitution of an invertebrate mass of lines that are neither prose nor verse, remained behind.

But this has nothing to do with Shakespeare, who certainly cannot be held responsible for the mishaps

of those who would walk in his circle without knowing the secrets of his magic. Of that magic his
manipulation of all verse that he tried—sonnet,
stanza, couplet, lyric, what not—is, perhaps, the
capital example, but it reaches its very highest point
in regard to blank verse. And, after all, it may be
wrong to use the word 'capital' even in regard to this.
For he is the *caput* throughout, in conception and in
execution, in character and in story—not an unnatural, full-blown marvel, but an instance of genius
working itself up, on precedent and by experiment,
from promise to performance and from the part to
the whole.

II

POEMS

INTRICATE as are the complications which have been introduced into the study of Shakespeare's plays by attempts to use them as supplements to the missing biography, they are as nothing to those which concern the non-dramatic poems, especially the *Sonnets*. The main facts, with which we shall begin, are by no means enigmatical; and, save in regard to the small fringe or appendix of minor pieces—*A Lover's Complaint*, and the rest—there can be no doubt of their authenticity, except in the minds of persons who have made up their minds that, as Shakespeare cannot possibly have written Shakespeare's works, somebody else must have done so. Something has been said in the preceding chapter concerning these poems, in connection with what is known of the general course of Shakespeare's life, and with the plays; but it seems expedient to treat them also, and more fully, by themselves.

Venus and Adonis, the earliest published, was licensed on 18 April 1593, and appeared shortly afterwards with a fully signed dedication by the author to the earl of Southampton, in which he describes the poem as 'the first heire of my invention'. It was followed a year later by *Lucrece*, again dedicated to Southampton. Both poems were very popular, and were praised (sometimes with the author's name mentioned) by contemporaries. Four years later, again, the invaluable Meres referred, in the famous passage about the plays, to their author's 'sugared sonnets among his private friends' as well as to *Venus* and *Lucrece*; and, a year later still, in 1599, Jaggard the printer included two of these sonnets, numbers 138 and 144, in *The Passionate Pilgrim*. The whole was not published till ten years later, in 1609, by Thomas Thorpe, with Shakespeare's full name, but without any dedication or other sign of recognition from him. The circumstances make it quite clear that Shakespeare did not wish to undertake any ostentatious responsibility for the publication; but it is, perhaps, rather rash to assume that this publication was carried out against his will or even without his privity. There is no evidence on either point; and the probabilities must be estimated according to each man's standard of the probable. What is certain is that he never repudiated them.

Thorpe subjoined to them *A Lover's Complaint*, about which we know nothing more. But, in *The Passionate Pilgrim*, Jaggard had not merely included the two sonnets referred to, but had assigned the whole of the poems, of which three others were actually taken from *Love's Labour's Lost*, to 'W. Shakespeare'. Others had already appeared under the names of Marlowe, Ralegh, Barnfield, Griffin and others. Nine have no further identification. It appears that, in this instance, Shakespeare did protest; at any rate, the dramatist Thomas Heywood, from whom Jaggard, in a later edition, 'lifted' two more poems to add to the original twenty, says that Shakespeare was 'much offended'—a little piece of evidence of a wide ranging effect, both positive and negative, which, perhaps, has never been quite fully appreciated.

Some of the *adespota* are quite worthy of Shakespeare; and his 'offence' would, of course, be quite sufficiently explained by the imputation to him of plagiarism from such men as the living Ralegh, and the dead Marlowe. Lastly, there exists a rather obscure, very curious and, in parts, extremely beautiful, poem called *The Phoenix and the Turtle*, which, in 1601, was added to Robert Chester's *Love's Martyr*, as a contribution by Shakespeare: Jonson, Chapman, 'Ignoto' and others contributing likewise. This was reprinted ten years later, and we hear of no protests on the part of any of the supposed contributors, though, whatever Shakespeare might be, neither Jonson nor Chapman could be described as 'gentle' or likely to take a liberty gently. We may take it, then, that, as regards the two classical pieces, the *Sonnets*, *A Lover's Complaint* and *The Phoenix and the Turtle*, we have at least the ordinary amount of testimony to genuineness, and, in the case of the first three, rather more than this; while some of *The Passionate Pilgrim* pieces are certainly genuine, and more may be. *Sonnets to Sundry Notes of Music*, it should, perhaps, be mentioned, though they often are separately entered in the contents of editions, merely form a division, with sub-title, of *The Passionate Pilgrim*.

There is nothing, therefore, so far, in what may be called the external and bibliographical history of the work, which justifies any special diversion from the study of it as literature. But, beyond all question, there is perilous stuff of temptation away from such study in the matter of the *Sonnets*. And, unfortunately, Thomas Thorpe stuck a burning fuse in the live shell of this matter by prefixing some couple of dozen words of dedication: 'To the only begetter of these ensuing sonnets Mr W. H. all happiness and that eternity promised by our ever-living poet wisheth the well-wishing adventurer in setting forth T. T.' It would be rash to guess, and impossible to calculate, how many million words of comment these simple nouns and verbs have called forth. The present writer has never seen any reason to abandon what has been, on the whole, the view most generally accepted by those who have some knowledge of Elizabethan literature and language, that this may be translated 'T. T., publisher of these sonnets, wishes to the sole inspirer of them, Mr W. H., the happiness and eternity promised by Shakespeare.' Moreover, though feeling no particular curiosity about the identification of 'Mr W. H.', he has never seen any argument fatal to that identification with William Herbert, earl of Pembroke, which has also been usual[1]. He admits, however, the possibility that 'W. H.' may be designedly inverted for 'H. W.' and that this may be Henry Wriothesly, earl of Southampton, which would bring the three great poem units into line. Nor, without attempting an

[1] The present fashion is to favour the Earl of Southampton rather than the Earl of Pembroke as the subject of the *Sonnets*.

impossible summary of theories and arguments on this head, must we omit to mention that there is one, commanding the support of Sidney Lee, to the effect that 'Mr W. H.''s 'begetting' had nothing whatever to do with the inspiration of the *Sonnets*; and that he himself was merely a sort of partner in their commercial production. And so, having solidly based the account of the poems on known facts and known facts only, let us pursue it in reference to their actual contents and literary character.

The author could hardly have chosen a happier sub-title for *Venus and Adonis* than 'first heire of [his] invention'. It is exactly what a child of youth should be, in merit and defect alike; though, as is always the case with the state of youth when it is gracious, the merits require no allowance, and the defects are amply provided with excuse. In general class and form, it belongs to a very large group of Elizabethan poetry, in which the combined influence of the classics, of Italian and, to a less degree, of recent French, literature are evident. For the particular vehicle, Shakespeare chose the sixain of decasyllabic lines riming *ababcc* which had been used by Spenser for the opening poem of *The Shepheards Calender*. This, like its congeners the rime royal and (in its commonest form) the octave, admits of that couplet or 'gemell', at the end which, as we know directly from Drayton and indirectly from the subsequent history of English prosody, was exercising an increasing fascination on poets. It is, perhaps, the least effective of the three, and it certainly lends itself least of all to the telling of a continuous story. But Shakespeare's object was less to tell a story than to draw a series of beautiful and voluptuous pictures in mellifluous, if slightly 'conceited', verse; and, for this, the stanza was well enough suited. As for the voluptuousness, it stands in need of very little comment either in the way of blame or in the way of excuse. The subject suggested it; the time permitted if it did not positively demand it; and there is evidence that it was not unlikely to give content to the reader to whom it was dedicated. If it were worth while it would be easy to show, by comparison of treatments of similar situations, that Shakespeare has displayed his peculiar power of 'disinfecting' themes of this kind even thus early. 'He who takes it makes it' is nowhere truer than of such offence as there may be in *Venus and Adonis*.

Its beauties, on the other hand, are intrinsic and extraordinary. Much good verse—after the appearance of 'the new poet' (Spenser) thirteen, and that of his masterpiece three, years earlier—was being written in this last decade of the sixteenth century. As was pointed out in the summary of prosody from Chaucer to Spenser[1], the conditions of rhythm, in accordance with the current pronunciation of English, had been at length thoroughly mastered. But, in Spenser himself, there are few things superior— in Drayton and Daniel and Sidney there are few things equal—at this time, to such lines as

Ten kisses short as one, one long as twenty,

[1] See *Camb. Hist. of Eng. Lit.* vol. III, chap. XIII.

or as

Leading him prisoner in a red-rose chain,

or the passages which have been wisely pounced
upon by musicians, 'Bid me discourse', and 'Lo!
here the gentle lark', with many others. To pass
from mere melody of line and passage to colour and
form of description, narrative, address and the like:
the pictures of the hare and of the horse and of the
boar, the final debate of the pair before Adonis
wrenches himself away, the morning quest—these
are all what may be called masterpieces of the novitiate, promising masterpieces of the mastership very
soon. If some are slightly borrowed, that is nothing.
It is usual in their kind; and the borrowing is almost
lost in the use made of what is borrowed. Naturally,
this use does not, as yet, include much novelty of
condition, either in point of character, or of what
the Greeks called *dianoia*—general cast of sentiment
and thought. It is a stock theme, dressed up with a
delightful and largely novel variety of verse and
phrase, of description and dialogue. But it is more
charmingly done than any poet of the time, except
Spenser himself, could have done it; and there is a
certain vividness—a presence of flesh and blood and
an absence of shadow and dream—which hardly the
strongest partisans of Spenser, if they are wise as
well as strong, would choose, or would in fact wish,
to predicate of him.

It has been usual to recognise a certain advance
in *Lucrece*; which was thus entitled at its publication,
though it had been licensed as *The Ravishment of*

Lucrece and has, later, been generally called *The Rape of Lucrece*. The reasons for this estimate are clear enough. There is the natural presumption that, in the case of so great a genius, there will be an advance; and there is the character, and, to some extent, the treatment, of the subject. This latter still busies itself with things 'inconvenient', but in the purely grave and tragic manner, the opportunities for voluptuous expatiation being very slightly taken, if not deliberately refused. The theme, as before, is a stock theme; but it is treated at greater length, and yet with much less merely added embroidery of description and narrative, which, at best, are accidentally connected with the subject. There is little pure ornament in *Lucrece* and a great deal of the much desiderated and applauded 'high seriousness', 'thoughtfulness' and the like. Moreover, to suit his more serious subject, Shakespeare has made choice of a more serious and ambitious vehicle—the great rime royal, which had long been the staple form of English poetry for serious purposes. The special qualities of this stanza, as it happens, are especially suited to such a theme as that of *Lucrece*; for, while it can do many things, its character of plangency— not for monotonous wailing but for the varied expression of sorrow and passion—had been magnificently shown by Chaucer and by Sackville. Nor is Shakespeare unequal to the occasion. The first two stanzas weave the more complicated harmony of rhythm and rime in which the septet has the advantage over the sixain to excellent effect; and there are fine examples later. The length of the piece—1854 lines—is neither excessive nor insufficient; the chief, if not the only, episode (Lucrece's sad contemplation of the painted tale of Troy) is not irrelevant, and is done almost as vigorously as the best things in *Venus and Adonis*. And, if the unbroken sadness of the piece, which is not disguised even in the overture, is oppressive, it can hardly be said to be unduly oppressive.

On the whole, however, while allowing to it an ample success of esteem, it is difficult to put it, as evidence of genius and as a source of delight, even on a level with *Venus and Adonis*, much more to set it above that poem. It is a better school exercise, but it is much more of a school exercise, much more like the poems which were being produced by dozens in the hotbed of late Elizabethan poetic culture. Though it is half as long again, it contains far fewer single lines or line batches of intense and consummate beauty than the *Venus*. Though there is more thought in it, there is less imagery, and even less imagination; the prosodic capacities (higher as they have been granted to be) of line and stanza are less often brought out; the greater equality of merit is attained by lowering the heights as well as by filling up the depths. What is specially remarkable, in the work of the greatest character monger and character master of all time, Lucrece is still very little of a *person*—rather less (one feels inclined to say) than either the lovesick goddess or her froward lover. She is a pathetic and beautiful type; she does and says nothing that is inappropriate to her hapless situation and much that is exquisitely appropriate; but she is not individualised. In short, the whole thing has rather the character of a verse theme, carefully and almost consummately worked out according to rule and specification by a very clever scholar, than that of the spontaneous essay of a genius as yet unformed. From *Venus and Adonis* alone, a cautious but well instructed critic might have expected either its actual later sequel of immensely improved work or, perhaps, though less probably, nothing more worth having. From *Lucrece*, the legitimate critical expectation would be, at best, a poet something like Drayton, but, perhaps, a little better, a poet whose work would be marked by power sometimes reaching almost full adequacy and competence, but rarely transcending, a poet somewhat deficient in personal intensity himself and still more in the power of communicating it to his characters and compositions.

Almost everyone who has any interest in literature is more or less acquainted with the interminable theories and disputes which have arisen on the subject of the *Sonnets*. Yet it should not be very difficult for anyone who has some intelligence to divest himself sufficiently of this acquaintance to enable him to read them as if they were a new book—uncommented, unintroduced, with nothing but its own contents to throw light or darkness upon it. If they are thus read, in the original order (for long after Shakespeare's death this order, purposely or not, was changed, though modern editions usually, and rightly, disregard this change), certain things will strike the careful reader at once. The first is that, by accident or design, the pieces composing the series are sharply, but very unequally, divided in subject, design being, on further inspection, pretty clearly indicated by the fact that the dividing point, sonnet 126, is not a sonnet at all, but a *douzain*. In this reading, it will, also, have become clear that the direct and expressed object of most of the first and far larger batch is a man, and that those of this batch which do not specify person or sex fall in with the others well enough; while the main object of the last and smaller batch is a woman. The first score or so of the earlier group, though containing expressions of passionate affection, are mainly, if not wholly, occupied with urging the person addressed to marry. Both batches contain repeated complaint—though it is not always exactly complaint—that the friend has betrayed the poet with the mistress and the mistress with the friend. (It is, however, perhaps, possible to argue that the identity of friend and mistress in the two batches is not proved to demonstration.) A large portion of the whole—perhaps nearly a third—is full of that half abstract, and almost impersonal, meditation on the joys and sorrows of love which is the special matter of the sonnet. One or two special and particular points, however, emerge—such as the indication of jealousy of other poets in respect of the friend, expressions of dissatisfaction with the writer's 'public means' of living or profession (which, most probably, is the actor's, but, it must be observed, far from necessarily so), and, in regard to the mistress, special, and repeated, insistence on the fact of her being a 'dark lady' with black eyes and hair. There is a good deal of wordplay on the name 'Will', which, of course, it would be absurd to overlook, but which had rather less significance in those days than it would have now.

All these things are quite unmistakable. That the friend was a 'person of quality' is generally admitted, and need not be much cavilled at, though it must be observed that the words 'so fair a house', in sonnet 13, do not necessarily bear the meaning of 'family'. But everything beyond is matter of doubt and question; while the very points just enumerated, though unmistakable in themselves, suggest doubt and question, to those who choose to entertain them, almost *ad infinitum*. Who was the friend? Pembroke, Southampton, or another? Who was the lady? Mistress Mary Fitton (who seems to have been a love of Pembroke, but who, they say, was fair, not dark) or somebody else? Who was the rival poet? When the list of uncertain certainties is overstepped, and men begin to construct out of the *Sonnets* a history of the course of untrue love in both cases, and endeavour to extend this history into something like a cipher chronicle of a great part of Shakespeare's life, we have, obviously, passed into cloudland. There is no limit to the interpretations possible to a tolerably lively fancy; and the limitless becomes more infinitely unlimited in respect to the criticisms and countercriticisms of these interpretations themselves.

On the other hand, it is possible to lay rather too much stress on the possibility of there being no interpretation at all or very little, of the *Sonnets* being merely, or mainly, literary exercises. It is, of course, perfectly true that the form, at this time, was an extremely fashionable exercise; and, no doubt, in some cases, a fashionable exercise merely. It is further true that, great as are the poetical merits and capacities of the sonnet, historically it has been, and from its nature was almost fated to be, more the prey of 'common form' than almost any other variety of poetic composition. The overpowering authority of Petrarch started this common form; and his Italian and French successors, enlarging it to a certain extent, stereotyped and conventionalised it even still more. It is perfectly possible to show, and has been well shown by Sidney Lee, that a great number, perhaps the majority of sonnet phrases, sonnet thoughts, sonnet ornaments, are simply coin of the sonnet realm, which has passed from hand to hand through Italian, French and English, and circulates in the actual Elizabethan sonnet like actual coin in the body politic or like blood in the body physical. All this is true. But it must be remembered that all poetry deals more or less in this common form, this common coin, this circulating fluid of idea and image and phrase, and that it is the very *ethos*, nay, the very essence, of the poet to make the common as if it were not common. That Shakespeare does so here again and again, in whole sonnets, in passages, in lines, in separate phrases, there is a tolerable agreement of the competent. But we may, without rashness, go a little further even than this. That Shakespeare had, as, perhaps, no other man has had, the dramatic faculty, the faculty of projecting from himself things and persons which were not himself, will certainly not be denied here. But whether he could create and keep up such a presentation of apparently authentic and personal passion as exhibits itself in these *Sonnets* is a much more difficult question to answer in the affirmative. The present writer is inclined to echo seriously a light remark of one of Thackeray's characters on a different matter: 'Don't think he could do it. Don't think anyone could do it'.

At the same time, it is of the first importance to recognise that the very intensity of feeling, combined, as it was, with the most energetic dramatic quality, would, almost certainly, induce complicated disguise and mystification in the details of the presentment. It was once said, and by no mere idle paradoxer, that the best argument for the identity of the dark lady and Mary Fitton was that Mistress Fitton, apparently, was a blonde. In other words, to attempt to manufacture a biography of Shakespeare out of the *Sonnets* is to attempt to follow a will-o'-the-wisp. It is even extremely probable that a number, and perhaps a large number, of them do not correspond to any immediate personal occasion

124

at all, or only owe a remote (and literally occasional) impulse thereto. The strong affection for the friend; the unbounded, though not uncritical, passion for the lady; and the establishment of a rather unholy 'triangle' by a cross passion between these two— these are things which, without being capable of being affirmed as resting on demonstration, have a joint literary and psychological probability of the strongest kind. All things beyond, and all the incidents between, which may have started or suggested individual sonnets, are utterly uncertain. Browning was absolutely justified when he laid it down that, if Shakespeare unlocked his heart in the *Sonnets*, 'the less Shakespeare he'. That the *Sonnets* testify to a need of partial unlocking, that they serve as 'waste' or overflow, in more or less disguised fashion, to something that was not unlocked, but which, if kept utterly confined, would have been mortal, may be urged without much fear of refutation. We see the heart (if we see it at all) through many thicknesses of cunningly coloured glass. But the potency and the variety of its operation are, however indistinctly, conveyed; and we can understand all the better how, when the power was turned into other, and freer, channels, it set the plays a-working.

To pass to more solid ground, the *Sonnets* have some mechanical, and many more not mechanical, peculiarities. The chief of the first class is a device of constantly, though not invariably, beginning with a strong caesura at the fourth syllable, and a tendency, though the sonnet is built up of quatrains alternately rimed with final couplet, to put a still stronger stop at the end of the second line (where, as yet, is no rime), and at each second line of these non-completed couplets throughout. The piece is thus elaborately built up or accumulated, not, as sonnets on the octave and sestet system often are, more or less continuously wrought in each of their two divisions or even throughout. This arrangement falls in excellently with the intensely meditative character of the *Sonnets*. The poet seems to be exploring; feeling his way in the conflict of passion and meditation. As fresh emotions and meditations present themselves, he pauses over them, sometimes entertaining them only to reject them or to qualify them later; sometimes taking them completely to himself. Even in the most artificial, such as sonnet 66, where almost the whole is composed of successive images of the wrong way of the world, each comprised in a line and each beginning with 'and', this accumulative character is noticeable; and it constitutes the strongest appeal of the greatest examples. While, at the same time, he avails himself to the full of the opportunity given by the English form for a sudden 'turn'—antithetic, it may be, or, it may be, rapidly summarising—in the final couplet. Of course, these mechanical or semi-mechanical peculiarities are not universal. He varies them with the same infinite ingenuity which is shown in his blank verse; so that, as for instance in the beautiful sonnet 71, the first two quatrains are each indissoluble, woven in one piece from the first syllable to the last. But the general characteristics have been correctly enough indicated in what has been said above.

Still, the attraction of the *Sonnets*, almost more than that of any other poetry, consists in the perpetual subduing of everything in them—verse, thought, diction—to the requirements of absolutely perfect poetic expression. From the completest successes in which, from beginning to end, there is no weak point, such as

> When to the sessions of sweet silent thought,

or

> Let me not to the marriage of true minds,

through those which carry the perfection only part of the way, such as

> When in the chronicle of wasted time,

down to the separate batches of lines and clauses which appear in all but a very few, the peculiar infusing and transforming power of this poetical expression is shown after a fashion which it has proved impossible to outvie. The precise subject (or, perhaps, it would be more correct to say the precise object) of the verse disappears. It ceases to be a matter of the slightest interest whether it was Mr W. H. or Mistress M. F. or anybody or nobody at all, so that we have only an abstraction which the poet chooses to regard as concrete. The best motto for the *Sonnets* would be one taken from not the least profound passage of the *Paradiso* of Dante

> *Qui si rimira nell' arte ch' adorna*
> *Con tanto affetto.*

127

And this admiration of the art of beautiful expression not only dispenses the reader from all the tedious, and probably vain, enquiries into particulars which have been glanced at, but positively makes him disinclined to pursue them.

The lesser poems, if only because of their doubtfulness, may be dealt with more shortly. *A Lover's Complaint*, by whomsoever written, must have been an early poem, but shows good powers in its writer. The rime royal, of which it is composed, is of the same general type as that of *Lucrece*, but has a few lines superior to any in the larger and more certain poem, such as the well-known last

> And new pervert a reconcilëd maid,

or the fine, and quite Shakespearean, second line in

> O father! what a hell of witchcraft lies
> In the small orb of one particular tear!

The jilted and betrayed damsel who is the heroine and spokeswoman has sparks of personal character. Of *The Passionate Pilgrim* pieces, not already known as Shakespeare's, or assigned to others, the two Venus and Adonis sonnets might be either suggested by the authentic poem to someone else or alternative studies for a different treatment of it by Shakespeare himself; and it is hardly possible to say of any of the rest that it cannot be, or that it must be, his. There are flashes of beauty in most of them; but, considering the way in which such flashes of beauty are shot and showered over and through the poetry of 1590—1610, this goes but a little way, or, rather, no way at all, towards identification. As for

The Phoenix and the Turtle, the extreme meta-
physicality of parts of it—

> Property was thus appalled
> That the self was not the same; etc.—

is by no means inconceivable in the Shakespeare of
Love's Labour's Lost and of some of the *Sonnets*. The
opening lines, and some of those that follow, are
exceedingly beautiful, and the contrast of melody
between the different metres of the body of the
poem and the concluding *threnos* is 'noble and most
artful'.

Inasmuch, moreover, as some of these minor and
doubtful pieces draw very close to the songs in the
plays, and actually figure in their company under
the thievish wand of Hermes-Jaggard, it cannot be
very improper to take them slightly into account,
with the songs and certainly assigned poems, as
basis for a short connected survey of Shakespeare's
poetical characteristics in non-dramatic verse. One
of these, which is extremely remarkable, and which
has been also noted in his dramatic verse, is the
uniform metrical mastery. This, when you come to
compare the two classical narratives, the *Sonnets* and
the songs with their possible companions among the
doubtful minors, is extraordinary. Neither Chaucer
nor Spenser was good at light lyrical measures,
admirable and beyond admiration as both were in
regard to non-lyrical verse, and accomplished, as
was at least Spenser, in the more elaborate and
slowly moving lyric. In fact, it may almost be said
that neither tried them. Shakespeare tries them

with perfect success; while his management of the sixain and septet is more than adequate, and his management of the English form of sonnet absolutely consummate. This lesser exhibition (as some would call it) of his universality—this universality in form —is surely well worth noting; as is, once more, the unusually lyrical character of some of his stanza work itself, and the likeness to his blank verse lines of not a few things both in stanza and in sonnet. This polymetric character has since become more and more common because poets have had examples of it before them. But it is first strongly noteworthy in Shakespeare.

Of the matter that he put into these forms, perhaps the first thing that ought to be remarked is that most of it certainly, and nearly all of it (except the later play songs) probably, dates from a very early period in his literary life; and the second, that the range of direct subject is not large. From this, enough having been said of the other productions, we may pass to the third observation: that in the *Sonnets* the absolute high water mark of poetry is touched, at least for those who believe with Patrizzi, and Hazlitt, and Hugo, that poetry does not so much consist in the selection of subject as in the peculiar fashion of handling the subject chosen. What their exact meaning may be is one question, with, as has been shown in practice, a thousand branches to it. It is a 'weary river', and, probably, there is no place where that river 'comes safe to sea' at all. Whether or not we wish, with Hallam, that they had never been written must be a result of the personal equation. But that, in the Longinian sense of the Sublime, they 'transport' in their finest passages as no other poetry does except the very greatest, and as not so very much other poetry does at all, may be said to be settled. If anyone is not transported by these passages, it is not impertinent to say that he must be like 'the heavier domestic fowls' of Dr Johnson's ingenious and effective circumlocution—rather difficult to raise by external effort and ill furnished with auxiliary apparatus for the purpose.

The poems other than the *Sonnets* are either tentative essays or occasional 'graciousnesses' for a special purpose; the *Sonnets* themselves have such an intensity of central fire that no human nature, not even Shakespeare's, could keep it burning, and surround it with an envelope able to resist and yet to transmit the heat, for very long. Fortunately, experiment and faculty both found another range of exercise which was practically unlimited; fortunately, also, they did not find it without leaving us record of their prowess in this.

CAMBRIDGE: PRINTED BY
WALTER LEWIS, M.A.
AT THE UNIVERSITY PRESS